our
ture
ooks
Bright

Your Future Looks Bright

Cheryl Walmsley

PEARSON
Prentice Hall
BUSINESS

Harlow, England • London • New York • Boston • San Francisco • Toronto • Sydney • Singapore • Hong Kong
Tokyo • Seoul • Taipei • New Delhi • Cape Town • Madrid • Mexico City • Amsterdam • Munich • Paris • Milan

PEARSON EDUCATION LIMITED

Edinburgh Gate
Harlow CM20 2JE
Tel: +44 (0)1279 623623
Fax: +44 (0)1279 431059
Website: www.pearsoned.co.uk

First published by the author under the Preston Beach imprint 2002
First published by Pearson Education in Great Britain in 2005

ISBN 0 273 70172 X

British Library Cataloguing in Publication Data
A CIP catalogue record for this book is available from the British Library

Library of Congress Cataloging-in-Publication Data
Walmsley, Cheryl.
    Your future looks bright/Cheryl Walmsley.
      p. cm.
    ISBN 0–273–70172–X (alk: paper)
      1. Job satisfaction. 2. Employees—Attitudes. 3. Organizational behavior. 4.
Self-management (Psychology) 5. Career development. I. Title.

HF5549.5.J63W22 2004
650.1—dc22

                                                           2004043172

10 9 8 7 6 5 4 3 2 1
09 08 07 06 05

Typeset in 10.5pt Iowan by 70
Printed and bound in Great Britain by Bell & Bain Ltd, Glasgow

The Publisher's policy is to use paper manufactured from sustainable forests.

For Michael and Timothy

Contents

Introduction

I know that work can be wonderful. The people you meet at work may inspire you and provide great company. The sense of achievement can be powerful and deeply satisfying. Work can teach you things and give you experiences that you never imagined. Work can be enormous fun.

And work can be awful. It's not difficult to become cynical through bad experiences or to lose respect for a particular employer. In some jobs it can be hard to believe that you're making a contribution, and there's no talent required in order to become miserable in a hurry.

Work can, of course, be somewhere between great and dreadful too. Few people have completely wonderful working days every day or totally awful ones. Our feelings about work can take on many shades but when it's a very dark grey, you might want to take some action.

It may be that you're already working or it may be you haven't started yet. Maybe you found yourself standing outside your workplace with a redundancy cheque in one hand, thinking, 'Now what?' Even without such prompting, a career crisis can hit at any time. You might one day ask yourself questions like 'Is this all there is? Is this what I really wanted to do with my life? Am I proud of myself when someone asks me what I do for a living? Do I make a living or submit to an existence? And if the pensions gloom is right, and if I'm going to be working until I'm 70, then is this what I see myself doing?'

When you look around you at the faces of people standing at the bus stop or waiting for the train doors to open, you might even think, 'OK, I'm not happy, but then, who is?'

That's settling for too little. You might need some time to think and some advice, but you don't need to have such low expectations for your working life.

This book has grown out of the work that I do in workplace motivation, change and development. I've seen a lot of people who've started out with unrealistic expectations and become disillusioned because they either expected too much or too little from work. And worse, there are too many people in jobs that never suited them, frustrated in the belief that they won't reach their potential or use their talents.

I've met many unhappy employees who have given up trying for enjoyment out of their work. They may believe that work satisfaction is a luxury reserved for a small minority. They may not know how to grab an opportunity or make a real change when it's needed. They may not know they're unwittingly contributing to the problem or that they don't understand the unwritten 'rules'.

There are some things you can't control but don't let that lull you into feeling completely helpless about your career. What you can do, right now, is make a decision to change your attitude. You do not have to sell your soul for work. Some people just stay in the rut they fall into. And you don't have to fall for the illusion that happiness is a goal to be pursued *one day* when you retire or win the lottery. The future is the day after this one. The future is the next few hours.

Life is short and work takes up a very large piece of it. Nothing should distract you from making changes so that you can enjoy your working life as much as possible. You can start over at any time by making a firm choice between two options: *Make a living or submit to an existence.*

If you pursue the former, then your future looks bright. And that's what this book is all about.

CHAPTER 1

HOW TO GET YOURSELF OUT OF A RUT

(or make sure you never get into one)

"No, I don't like work. I had rather laze about and think of all the fine things that can be done. I don't like work – no man does – but I like what is in the work – the chance to find yourself. Your own reality – for yourself, not for others – what no other man can ever know. They can only see the mere show, and never can tell what it really means."

Joseph Conrad – Heart of Darkness

You might not set out to change the world, but you *can* change your working life. You don't need to be in a state of constant excitement or wearing the fixed grin of an idiot to love your work. You're not required to sing the corporate anthem, salute the management team or pray in the general direction of head office each morning to be a valuable employee.

It is a pitiful waste of your life to do something, year in and year out, that you feel no satisfaction in, or love for.

You are not your job. You are many things, and work is only one aspect of your life. But here's a chilling thought – in a week of 168 hours, you'll probably have around 112 waking hours. You will probably spend around 50 per cent of the waking hours working, getting to and from work or thinking about work.

Again, you're NOT your job, but the proportion of your life that is taken up by work means that you can *feel* as if you are your job. It is a pitiful waste of your life to do something, year in and year out, that you feel no satisfaction in, or love for.

You'll probably *want* to work. Most people do and even the richest people will usually apply themselves to work of some kind. Few can be completely idle for long and find that to be a satisfying and happy existence.

❝Absence of occupation is not rest,
A mind quite vacant is a mind distressed.❞

Cowper

Let's be real – most of us have to work. But it doesn't follow that you should feel miserable about that. (We have to eat and not many of us hate food.) It isn't necessary just to tolerate your work and view it as something that pays the bills. You don't have to live for it and you don't have to suffer it either. In any case, life is too short to waste time feeling trapped, bored or short-changed by employment. Ideally, your chosen work should add to your life rather than keep you from it. If you tell someone what you do for a living, at the very least it ought to *feel* like living.

There are good reasons to stay very optimistic about work and the personal rewards it can bring. I know that can be hard sometimes. You may get distracted or frustrated. Anyone can allow the experience of a failure or a bad choice to dampen their spirit. You may fall for the idea that 'work is an endless cycle of misery and exploitation'. The question 'who do I think I am to expect a happy working life?' may cross your mind. You may allow others to 'convince' you that your life is not so special or that your time is not so valuable. Others can be awfully powerful and you can forget, in the foghorn of louder voices, how very strong and capable you are.

I believe that most people are freer than they choose to be and stronger than they realise. It is absolutely possible to feel good about what you do for a living – IF YOU WANT IT TO BE SO. You are capable of creating challenges and finding fun in whatever you choose to do. But you have to make some choices if you want to love your work. (Don't wait for permission to make a change. It's your life and you're in charge of it.) Life is short. Love the work you choose to do.

Make the decision to make the decisions

I was 15 years old, on a school excursion, staring at a large modern sculpture with my face screwed up. The sculpture resembled, I thought, a cross between a doughnut and something I should avoid stepping in. A boy in my class observed my scowl and asked me why I didn't like it. I was completely dismissive. 'Well! Just look at it! Anyone could have done that. Even I could have done that!' He looked at it for a moment and said, 'Yes, but YOU didn't, and THAT'S the difference.'

I haven't seen him for 20 years, but I can still register the impact of that important point; 'If you're not prepared to have a go, then *shut up*.'

Fast-forward a few years – I was in a lecture called 'The Social Psychology of Work'. The lecturer was explaining a theory called 'The Locus of Control'. 'People,' he said, 'tended to be **internals** or **externals**.' They either saw some connection between their own actions and what happened to them in life (internals) or they did *not* see such a link (externals).

The externals held outside forces such as luck, fate, the stars, other people's actions, bio-rhythms, or the government responsible for whatever their lives had become. But internals believed that if something was going to happen, they'd better get on and make it happen. An 'internal locus of control' was an inner voice that said, 'I'm in the driving seat.' For internals, success and happiness were goals to be worked towards rather than wishes granted by genies.

Internals seemed to come out as the more satisfied workers since they had a habit of doing something about situations where they weren't happy. Internals tended to come out as the preferred employees too, since they had a habit of taking responsibility.

'Hmm,' I thought. 'That's interesting.' I was 19. It reminded me of my classmate who had made me see the link between those who get up and do something and those who sit back and carp.

Fast-forward another 10 to 15 years and I no longer find this theory to be mildly diverting. The mental watershed, known as 'locus of control,' is something I work with and observe on a daily basis. Both extremes (internal and external) are very real to me now. I observe them both, viewing their lives and their working days through two very different kinds of lenses.

Internals say things like, 'Here's what I'm thinking', 'What can I do?', 'Let's get together and sort that out' or 'How can I help?' It's not that internals feel obliged to do all the thinking and working on their own. It's just that they're willing to *face realities and act*. Conversations tend to be more relevant and focused. Internals quickly feel patronized if they think you're trying to control them or tell them what to do. They're more inclined to work toward enjoying what they do. They're prepared to look in the mirror when the plan goes awry. Internals can't believe that people can see the world in any other way.

Externals, when complaining about their working lives, tend to demand in frustrated tones that something be done (usually by 'management'). Sometimes externals bitch about their lack of progress, sniping at the 'lucky ones' who are promoted or grumbling because 'work' hasn't treated them well.

There are some happy externals who land in a good place and are content to go with the flow. There are unhappy externals who say 'when I win the lottery' just a little too often. 'Que Sera, Sera' is their anthem. Externals can get offended if you suggest that they help themselves or if you fail to tell them what to do. Externals can't believe that people can see the world in any other way.

Externals may get distressed, wondering 'What's going to happen to me?' or 'What are the rumours today?' Internals tend to search for or even create opportunities, keep up their skills and take risks. Internals know that if they don't look after their careers, nobody else will.

 The sometimes shocking and difficult thing for all of us to accept is that success is largely about *our own attitudes and behaviours*. For many people, advice about work and success needs to contain quick-fix solutions, or else it's deemed 'unhelpful'. Realistic career management skills may sound unrealistic to people who want the magic trick.

Typically, externals respond with, 'That's all right for you, but in the real world . . .' kind of comments. And yet we're all living in the same 'real' world.

People with an internal locus of control get on with their lives and may not have the time, energy or patience to share their 'secrets' with the rest. That may sound selfish, but why should anyone care about your career – besides you? And why should anyone care about your career if you don't seem to?

Your career is very much within your influence. Of course, there are things that are beyond our influence and control. The weather, natural disasters, some misfortunes and tragedies, market forces, boardroom decisions and lottery results are amongst the things we can prepare for, but not completely control.

But your career is very much within your influence. There are always setbacks and frustrations and they happen to everyone. Internals can fail, feel pain, lose out and be hurt. Invariably they will get up again. That is not about being lucky. That is to do with strength, purpose and a clear distaste for lying down and wailing for too long.

"It is not the critic who counts; not the man who points out how the strong man stumbles or where the doer of deeds could have done better. The credit belongs to the man who is actually in the arena; whose face is marred by dust and sweat and blood; who strives valiantly, who errs and comes up short again and again, because there is no effort without error and shortcoming, but does actually strive to do the deeds; who does know the great

enthusiasms, the great devotions; who spends himself for a worthy cause; who at best, knows, in the end, the triumph of achievement, and who at the worst, if he fails, at least he fails while daring greatly, so that his place shall never be with those cold and timid souls who know neither victory nor defeat."

Theodore Roosevelt

If you want to love your work, you have to be willing to take control of your working life. This means joining those people who understand that there is a strong connection between their own actions and what happens, in life and in the workplace. You have to be in the arena and a 'doer of deeds', a person who tries and strives – a risk taker. You may even choose to 'dare greatly' with your own career. The alternative is to be among the 'cold and timid souls' who live in an employment rut, where there are no big wins, no big failures nor opportunities to love their work. 'Why doesn't someone', 'why don't they', 'could have', 'should have', 'would have' and 'if only' need to be put aside if you really want to get out of a rut and love your work.

If you want to change your life, I will not wish you good luck because I don't believe it's about that. Loving what you do for a living starts with making the decision to make the decisions.

Changes and Choices

If you're unhappy with your work, I must warn you that the odds are against a miracle rescue.

Everyone has bad days at work. Every job or career has some lows attached to it or some aspects that are not very appealing. Few, if any, employment situations can offer constant and relentless stimulation and learning.

But when the good days are very hard to identify and the reasons for staying are difficult to find, it may be time to make a decision. If you're asking yourself 'What am I doing here?' at least once a week, it's time. If you're wallowing in dreams of a lottery win to provide you with an escape, it's time. If you're wishing for a fire drill to give you a few minutes' break and some fresh air, it's time. If you have set off the fire alarm or made the hoax call – TRUST ME – it really is time to make a change!

Change is something that we can fear or crave, resist or pursue. Sometimes we can handle change with ease and sometimes we can go to pieces at the very mention of it.

The most difficult bit is to say, 'I want a change' or 'I need a change.' That's a start, but then there's the realization that you've got things to do. It's not likely that anyone is going to change your life for you and would you want that anyway? If you're unhappy and you know it, or if you think life could be better and the future could be brighter, here are your main choices.

- **Choice number 1.** You could try to change the existing situation. *Change the place you're in.*
- **Choice number 2.** You could move to a different situation. *Change your job or your work.*

- **Choice number 3.** You could *do nothing*. (Except *complain* to anyone who's prepared to listen.)

- **Choice number 4.** You could try to change your attitude, expectations and behaviour within the existing situation. *Change yourself.*

Below is an elaboration of these four choices. If you recognize one that's right for you immediately, you'll probably want to go straight to the chapters that relate directly to that choice. Just a word of caution here; many of us think the answer to our less-than-ideal work happiness is to change the job (Choice 2). And that may be true. However, you may change your job and discover that your working life is no better, because the job was only part of the problem.

The choices above aren't always 'either/or' – the answer can be a combination. Maybe you do need to change your job but maybe you also need to change yourself a little bit too. Maybe you should try to change the place you're in first?

It's very hard to accept that your own behaviour might be a contributing factor to the problem, but there will be no progress without honesty. If you can at least accept that possibility, and *genuinely* stop and think about it, then your working future is inevitably going to be brighter.

Choice number 1

Change the place you're in

How do you change your workplace? How big a change is required? Do you have the energy and the determination to do it? Do you care enough to do it? Are you prepared to not only rock the boat but to redesign it?

People DO make changes to their workplaces, through individual persistence, persuasion or group pressure. They may be small changes like rearranging the office for better space, or big changes like shifting the company's strategy. It may be something like introducing a charitable element to the work you do, to bring added satisfaction if that's what's lacking.

Changing the workplace is a somewhat heroic option. It might also be the crazy option. The gains may be enormous, but the risk is that you burn out trying while nothing changes very much. What if the change you think will improve the place actually makes it worse?

Or you may be experiencing some difficulty that is unique to you. Maybe the overtime that's expected is not possible for you or a particular task is causing grief. There may be a solution. Talk it through with your manager *at least*. If you're seen as a valuable employee and a change can be made for you, then you may not have to do anything drastic at all.

Don't simply take the problem to a manager. Managers hear enough problems. Managers are interested in people with ideas and solutions. Stay calm and be prepared with *well thought through proposals and alternatives*. Show that you've considered the problem and understand the constraints within the business.

Speak respectfully (and with good humour) to the people who can help you to bring about the change. Try not to attack, explode or imply that the decision maker's stupidity and inertia are to blame. That might be the case, but it's also possible that they're just as frustrated and aware of the situation as you are.

Be prepared to do it alone. The rousing chorus of support behind you may disappear as you reach the manager's door. True allies can be a bit thin on the ground and hard to count on. Resistance is a reality. Remember physics? For every action, there's an equal and opposing reaction.

Human beings tend to be cagey at having their routines altered even if they're not working. Habit is comfortable. Bad habits are comfortable. Accept resistance before you start. It may ease a bit of the frustration.

"The innovator makes enemies of all those who prospered under the old order and only lukewarm support is forthcoming from those who would prosper under the new."

Machiavelli

If you generally enjoy what you do but see a need for some things to change, then try to make that change. If you believe there is realistic hope for improvement and you don't want to move – then try. But be sure that you do or could love your work and genuinely believe in the outcome you are pursuing.

There is no progress without people who are prepared to act.

Choice number 2

Change your job or your work

If you're fed up with your work and can't see a way to make a meaningful change, improve things or adapt yourself to it, then *do all you can* to move on.

If you have good reason to believe that your efforts will *not* be rewarded or that there are very real barriers (rather than imagined ones) to your achieving success in this place, then it's probably wise to get out.

It is NOT a tragedy to leave a job or a career. Life is a journey forwards. Any job or career can be viewed as a chapter, or a stage. It is not life itself.

You have options. You could look for the same job with another employer. There's also self-employment as a freelancer, contractor or consultant. You could set up your own small business. You might be able to job-share, downshift, work part-time, do something voluntary, do a couple of different part-time jobs, work from home etc. You might even want to do something unrelated. You could change career entirely. You might head back to study.

You might even consider asking for some unpaid leave; a 'gap year' or a sabbatical, so you can think things over. It may not be the job after all. It's possible you're tired and need some time to think.

All these options require some homework but they're not 'pie in the sky'. Look around you. You already know people who have made those changes in their lives. Ask them about the lessons they learned and any advice they'd give you.

You may want to find another job before you leave the one you're in. That could be the wiser thing to do because most managers like to 'employ from the employed'. If the situation is really bad, however, you might bail out without your next move in place. People do it and survive.

But don't burn your bridges. Tempting as it is to break your middle fingers while waving goodbye, it's never a smart thing to do. Appealing as it sounds to give someone an honest earful – hold back. Leave with dignity. There is a process called reference checking that may go on formally or informally. You don't want anyone's anger to spoil your future chances. People are surprisingly good at remembering first *and last* impressions.

Advising you to leave your workplace may reek of treachery. Leaving may feel like giving up or losing. You may even feel indignant at this suggestion. 'Why should I be the one to leave?' 'If I leave, then they'll have won.'

I understand those reactions and I sympathize, but I've learned to have more respect for my own time, health and happiness. You MIGHT be trying your hardest and working your socks off. If there's a moral or technical battle going on, you MIGHT be in the right. But sometimes the effort is too much for one person and you can make yourself ill over something that *just isn't worth it.*

It may not be fair that you're the one who's leaving. Life is not always fair. Sometimes good things happen to the undeserving and horrible things happen to good people. It's not a perfect world. It's a challenge to remain reasonable and professional in all your dealings with people, but it's not a requirement that you stick out every work situation that you find yourself in.

Sometimes you can be in the wrong kind of workplace or culture for you. (Every workplace has a culture, or different habits and ways of doing things.) Sometimes you're in the wrong job or career. It doesn't mean you're a bad person or that you have failed. Perhaps the job was right for you once, but now YOU have changed. You'll find out what suits you and what doesn't. That's a learning process and it's a perfectly useful part of life.

It's OK to acknowledge your feelings about moving on. We do get attached to people and have memories of achievements and shared experiences. But don't let the past hold you back if the work isn't right for you anymore.

The security system is there to stop people from breaking in. *It's not there to stop you from breaking out!* There is no sniper on the roof, waiting to aim at you for daring to resign. Nobody's doing a fingerprint check on the situations vacant page. Vote with your feet. The place will carry on without you. Turnover is an accepted part of working life.

A good start would be to make a plan. Get a piece of paper and start planning a job change. This should result in some 'to do' items, like calls to make, places to search, people to speak to etc. It's not likely that a miracle offer will come along tomorrow, but how is *anything* going to happen if you do not act?

Choice number 3

Do nothing

Choice number 3 is a failure to consider the other three rational options. It is a failure to act at all, rather than a step towards change. Choice number 3 is the one I see a lot of people go for and I hope you're not amongst them.

There are lots of reasons why we can fail to act. Some are understandable and others less so. I can sympathize with the employee who believes they can't change because they feel helpless and unable to think through their situation and the options that they have.

Sometimes you can be just too tired to add a job search to your current pressures. I can understand that. I don't enjoy going to interviews. They shred the nerves of most people. Anyone of us can become too overwhelmed to add a change of workplace, commute, colleagues and challenges to the load. Asking for help is a good start.

Refusing to act, or feeling unable to act, might also be fuelled by an inner belief that 'my life is not within my hands' (externals!). Taking that a step further, 'controlling forces are to blame for my problem and are therefore responsible for the solution'. The news for externals is: you're wrong. Your working life *is* within your hands. Certainly your career choices are up to you. And while you may have been powerless in the face of a merger, decline, sell out, takeover, downsize or radical change in the workplace, YOU are choosing to stay there.

'They might make me redundant.'

This may be wise when such cutback plans are afoot and a voluntary scheme is on offer. But otherwise, playing 'wait and see' when you're very unhappy isn't wise. Looking for work when you absolutely must is a poor proposition. The search is a more desperate one, because the work you had has run out and you're not bargaining for a new job from a position of strength. You're now unemployed and your prospective employers know it. It raises the question 'Why was this person let go?' The better alternative is 'Why is this person seeking a change?'

I worked with a fellow called Jack who constantly whined and wished for a redundancy payout, though there was no plan for cutting staff at the time. If you asked Jack, 'How are you?' he would answer, 'I'll be all right when they make me redundant. I wish they'd hurry up.' (I wished they would too, but that's another story.)

I asked after Jack a few years ago and discovered that the company had, in fact, let him go. They'd fired him for a long-running embezzlement scam. Jack had turned his misery into a daily (and self-justified) habit of stealing. Of course he was caught. It reinforces my belief that sitting around in a job you hate is not good for you or the employer. (Acts of sabotage and fraud invariably come back to hurt the perpetrator most of all, but they hardly help the rest of the team.) No big payout for Jack! And had he been honest, he would by now, have received that elusive large payout.

'There isn't a job like mine in this area.'

I heard this repeatedly from an unhappy group who apparently thought they could find *exactly* the same role in *exactly* the same kind of organization, without changing their commute, salary or colleagues. Further to this delusion, the group expected a mythical employer to come and woo them. They'd done absolutely nothing about a job search.

'I've got a mortgage.'

So has most of the workforce. Mortgages are a practical reality and finances must be considered, but financial arrangements are a choice that you make. Having a mortgage is not a barrier to looking for work alternatives. People move jobs and rearrange finances every day with a minimum of fuss. It is doable. Some mortgages even give payment breaks.

'This is where I live. I've got family here.'

Moving a family is not impossible. Many have done it and managed to survive and thrive. A difference of a few miles is piddling. Some people move thousands of miles and face isolation, hardship and extreme cultural change.

When unhappy employees cite their families as a reason why they must stay put, I ask whether they've ever had a serious discussion at home about how they're feeling. A daily whine is not a genuine conversation. Of course, it's a big proposition and needs care and planning, but it's very doable. Moving to a new place and starting over could turn out to be the best thing that's ever happened to you.

'I don't have that skill. I can't compete in today's market.'

'Not having a skill' is more of a challenge than a reasonable excuse. Why not go and get it? Adult education is often widely available and sitting there waiting to be used. Your current employer may be very willing to support your desire for the updated skill. (Shrewd employers know they'll benefit!) Ask for training advice. Make enquiries about the costs and availability. Of course, an employer is not very likely to fund pottery lessons if their business is merchant banking, but many companies will help with fees, books or even study leave. *It is worth asking.* The worst reaction you might hear is 'no', and that won't kill you. It's not likely that what you've learned by the end of your adolescence will be enough to see you through your working life. Learning and development is an ongoing process.

'I'm too old' or 'I'm not old enough.'

'I'm getting older. Therefore I'm trapped!' If you're getting older, you have a greater reason to seize the day and make the most of your working life. Of course, the prejudice against older employees can exist, so you have good reasons to make sure your skills and experiences are attractive to new employers. Don't undervalue your experiences and the results you have achieved.

I've heard people use both youth and seniority as excuses for not managing their own careers. Age is just a fact. Some people might use it as a reason to doubt you, but usually that happens if they sense you're not too sure of yourself. Try not to make it a barrier in your own mind when you're managing your working life. Just think about all the people who have pursued their goals in spite of age or youth.

There can also be a prejudice against youth. If you're still relatively young, don't undervalue your enthusiasm and desire to learn. These are also attractive qualities to employers.

Marking time doesn't help

I once felt trapped in an unhappy work situation, and gave myself a time limit, like a prisoner making scratches on a wall. I don't recommend this to anyone. Work should never feel like a prison.

I have encountered very few genuine examples of employees being stuck. And those I observed were not unhappy with their work. They had found ways to cope and enjoy the day. They may have lowered their expectations or simply found ways to challenge themselves and have fun. Chronic unemployment, severely limited opportunities and unusual personal commitments might create such circumstances.

I know that I'd be unwilling to move, in the short term, if I was very close to a real benefit, like a bonus that would be forfeited by my move. I wouldn't want to walk away from a significant reward that I felt I'd earned. Even so, the short term shouldn't be expressed in years.

Back to the reasons for doing nothing; there are a few bad habits that are a bit harder to sympathize with. The following destructive beliefs can keep you in a holding pattern of inaction – apathy, complaining and martyrdom.

→ Apathy

The comfort zone is where consistency rules, and risks are avoided at all cost. This zone is an overcrowded, boring place. You might be tempted to live without risk, in the belief that you can keep change from touching you, but you're kidding yourself. You can't lock change out. The comfort zone is also called the dead zone. To quit a job mentally, but stay in it physically, is to occupy the 'dead zone' in employment. Please don't let this be you.

The sad fact is that apathy is a hybrid weed that grows from laziness and comfort. I'd like a dollar for every unhappy employee who shrugged at me and said, 'The devil you know is better than the devil you don't'. It isn't.

"Life is either a daring adventure or nothing. Security does not exist in nature, nor do the children of men as a whole experience it. Avoiding danger is no safer in the long run than exposure."

Helen Keller

→ Complaining

Also known as whining, grizzling, grumbling, moaning and bleating, complaining is often countered in workplaces with phrases such as 'Not that again' or 'What are you on about now?' or 'Oh for God's sake – not this again, please!'

If people tend to walk away from you when you're talking, it's possible you may have inadvertently joined those unhappy, lip-curling serial whiners, who seem to enjoy their misery and believe that complaining is a normal way of conversing with people. This is the 'awfully glad to be unhappy' brigade. Constant carping about problems without acting usefully can become a way of life.

You'll also know if you've become a serial whiner if you don't take a real interest in solving your problem. If you switch off and sneer when people try to say something helpful, if you play 'yes but' when you hear any ideas at all, then the job isn't the problem. Someone with a real desire for change leans forward and starts talking through possibilities.

→ Martyrdom

You have unfortunately become a bit of a work martyr if you tend to use comments such as 'I've been kicked around for twenty years by this company' or 'I've been through hell in this job' or 'You've got no idea what I've put up with here!' If you find it strange when people suggest you move on and say things like 'Well, what if we all got up and left?' or 'I feel I owe it to the company' or 'Who says we're meant to enjoy our work?' or even 'What about loyalty?' then you are quite possibly slipping into a bad habit of confusing work with a sentence that must be served.

There is no Olympic gold medal for 'suffering at work' or giving long service to an employer you detest or doing a job you don't enjoy. If you're staying in the belief that your devotion and suffering is admired by all and crucial to the survival of the place, then please make a move. As a colleague once said to a martyr, 'Get off the cross; someone else needs the wood!'

If you feel you're doing nothing and it really is time to do something – then take some time to think about why you have stalled. What is *really* holding you back? And when you've confronted the reasons for the inaction, make a vow to yourself to act and move forward and get some support from others. It's very likely that the people around you can identify the barriers you put in front of yourself. It's pretty likely they've heard you say it all out loud.

Choice number 4

Change yourself

Changing yourself is a brave and difficult thing to do. It requires that you admit you might be your own worst enemy.

It's a big person who will admit that they need to work on themselves, but the results of taking action can be incredible. Even the most successful people, indeed, probably the most successful people, are capable of continuously asking themselves if they are doing the best they could and if a new approach or attitude might help.

You have to stop being defensive about the way you are. Nobody's perfect. You have flaws and faults. You have weaknesses. You also have strengths and talents. It is a relief to see yourself in a more rational and human light.

You can start exploring possibilities for change when you are honest about what needs to change. It doesn't mean you have to become a different person – rather you are confronting how some of your behaviours might be holding you back. Maybe you do not make enough of your strengths.

Having the courage to change your own behaviour can have a remarkable knock-on effect on other people's reactions towards you. It encourages other people to relax a bit and be honest about themselves too.

Facing this choice takes some insight and willpower. It means asking people who will be honest with you and listening to what they say, without interruption. They may not be right, but do you hear any patterns or consistent themes from amongst your pool of friends and colleagues?

You need to take a good look at yourself and really understand the 'thing' you're doing that is letting you down. Then, you need to do some hard work to change that behaviour and stop yourself reverting back to the old habit. This is all much easier to say than it is to do.

So, how do you know if it's YOU? Let's say that you're unhappy and not producing the work you know you're capable of. Here are some questions that require honest answers:

- Have you ever been happy at any work?
- Was there a significant length of time when you performed at consistently higher levels?

- Are you generally described as self-motivated and positive in your outlook?

- Are you usually considered to be a valuable employee?

- Are you trusted with confidential work matters?

- Is your opinion asked for?

- Is there widespread disillusionment amongst the more respected and professional employees? (Don't look at the whiners – they're always in the pits!)

If you have answered a few *noes* to these questions, then it may be time to take a long look in the mirror. Moving to another place might not change the problem that is fuelling your unhappiness.

Now try these questions:

- Has anyone commented on a change (for the worse) in your behaviour?

- Have you been passed over for opportunities that you felt you deserved?

- Do you feel a little ashamed of yourself sometimes?

- Are you starting to play games?

- Have you been sabotaging anything or anyone, deliberately tripping people up?

- Do you feel unwilling and unable to offer any positive suggestions because you hate the place so much?

- Have you turned people away from doing business with your workplace?

Are you coming up with a lot of *yes* answers? If so, you need to act before you are acted upon, and before your own unhappiness pulls you down.

Consistent *underachievement* at work can lead to being fired – slowly or quickly. That's hardly a barrel of laughs. And whose name is most likely to be at the top of the list if cutbacks occur? Some managers wait for an excuse like 'across the board reductions' to get rid of the 'guy with the attitude problem'.

You may decide that you want to make some changes to your behaviour *and* change jobs too. A fresh start can be good, but you don't *have* to leave. I've seen people turn around their own behaviour and remain within the same job. Frank admission of their own problem ('I went through a bad time') and support from others enabled them to stay and get back on track. Promotions aren't necessarily denied if you can go through a slump and come out on the positive side.

What about boredom? Is the work so boring (to you) that you can't see a way to have any fun with it? Or are you lacking in the personal energy and enthusiasm to have some fun? There's no such thing as a boring job. You can always find someone who has turned a boring job into fun or some kind of challenge. Similarly, there are individuals who whine 'I'm bored' no matter where they are. It may be that the work situation isn't right for you or it may be that your own attitude needs a kick-start.

OK, I need to change – what's the first BIG step?

You will change the situation only when you acknowledge your own behaviour and decide that you want to make a positive change. *And no one can do that for you.*

Many people will help and would be pleased to be asked, but that first push must come from you. This is true for any behavioural problem – from drug addiction to nail-biting. Denial can be very comfortable. It could take you too long to face the need to change.

"Three things make people want to change. One is that they hurt sufficiently. They have beaten their heads against the same wall for so long that they decide they have had enough. They have invested in the same slot machines without a pay-off for so long that they are finally willing either to stop playing or to move on to others. Their migraines hurt. Their ulcers bleed. They are alcoholic. They have hit the bottom. They beg for relief. THEY WANT TO CHANGE.

Another thing that makes people want to change is a slow type of despair called ennui, or boredom. This is what the person has who goes through life saying 'so what' until he finally asks the ultimate big 'so what'. HE IS READY TO CHANGE.

A third thing that makes people want to change is the SUDDEN DISCOVERY THAT THEY CAN."

Thomas Harris

This sudden discovery, that we *choose* the way we behave – the things we say and do, is an interesting thing to observe.

This 'aha' moment comes with words like, 'You know, that's right. I *do* choose my behaviour', 'I *can* change', 'I *can* be different', 'I *can* make choices', 'I don't have to put up with this', 'I *am* free to do what I like and live with the consequences', 'I am responsible and accountable', 'I do not have to be here', 'I do not have to accept this situation' and 'What the hell was I waiting for?'

We *choose* the way we behave – the things we say and do.

Everyone is free to make this sudden discovery and use this invisible key to life. We're also free to ignore it and play the victim. There is a moment of choice in everything, and that knowledge is not possessed by all.

If you've seen the film *When Harry Met Sally*, you might recall how Billy Crystal sprinted to find Meg Ryan on New Year's Eve. He couldn't wait to ask her to marry him. He said, 'When you realize you want to spend the rest of your life with somebody, you want the rest of your life to start as soon as possible.'

It's the same reaction for those who make the sudden discovery that they CAN change and that they CAN choose their behaviour. They want the rest of their life to start now. They don't want to go back.

I do recall the point in my own life when I was confronted by this new kind of talk. The questions fired at me were, 'Who chooses your behaviour? Who is in charge of your life? Who controls your actions and reactions?' There was a part of me that flinched. Part of me felt annoyed and irritated.

Even more irritating, the interrogator refused to budge an inch on personal accountability.

"The truth that makes men free is for the most part the truth which men prefer not to hear."

Hagar

Of course, adopting this accountable, or internal, attitude is not all beer and skittles. Life is not suddenly perfect just because you decide to take more control over it. Things will happen that you have little control over. You don't shut down your feelings and become invincible. You need to reserve the right to be angry. You don't have to become a doormat, perfectly accepting and putting up with anything others might care to dish out. There is a BIG difference between autonomy (having power over self) and being an automation.

But a small warning if you go ahead and make a positive change in your own behaviour or, indeed, in your life. Changing work and explaining the move by saying 'I wasn't happy' can produce a funny kind of backlash. Why?

When a person changes their life and their behaviour, it shows that it can be done. It can make those who play 'wait and see – not up to me' a little uncomfortable. Some people may not like to see the proof that change is possible or that goals can be achieved. They might make fun of the person who is trying, the 'man who is in the arena', not because the situation is funny, but because they are uncomfortable with the evidence before their eyes. It's a nervous kind of laugh.

'If the problem was MY behaviour, surely someone would have told me.' Don't hold your breath waiting for unprompted feedback.

Even the feedback you ask for can be very guarded. People worry about being honest and may tell you only the trivial or obvious things you know already. Some people may be worried about your reaction. Fears of confrontation, loss of control or a vindictive strike can mean that important words are held back. Who would go out of their way to have a serious talk with someone who was unhappy with their work? It might fall under the manager's role, but managers can shy from these talks.

We all have options for change, although 'doing nothing' is not much of a choice. To take a line from *The Shawshank Redemption*, 'I guess it comes down to a simple choice. You get busy living or you get busy dying.' Change is not a miracle that you should sit around and wish for. A real and lasting change in your life is not 'done' to you by some rescuing force.

❝The greatest discovery of my generation is that a man can alter his life by altering his attitudes.❞

William James

Change starts with self-awareness and sincerity. It is achieved through effort and persistence. We might shy away from the idea of real change because of these words *effort* and *persistence*. I hope they don't scare you.

Misery loves company and you'll always find someone who is as unhappy as you are. Don't let that lull you into a state of apathy and inertia. You can always change **your** world.

CHAPTER 2

A QUICK GUIDE TO THINGS THAT DON'T CHANGE

no matter what you do,
where you work or who you are

"Give me the serenity to accept the things I cannot change, courage to change the things I can and the wisdom to know the difference."

Attributed to Reinhold Niebuhr

A great deal of frustration and unhappiness will come from bashing your head against brick walls. You can switch jobs every few months and still not find what you're looking for. And it may be that it doesn't exist *anywhere* (unless maybe you leave organizational life to work for yourself – and possibly not even then). It may also be true that great opportunities lie waiting in the places where *you can make a difference*. Knowing the changeable from the unyielding is going to save a lot of time and energy. Knowing the two apart also helps you to pick up and carry on when you hit the obstacles.

This chapter could also be called 'the harsh realities about work' because there are some things that don't change – no matter what kind of work you do. It's about adjusting your expectations to the realistic so that you are not endlessly disappointed, chewing your knuckles and wondering why the world doesn't dance to your tune.

Many a forehead has been scraped, mine included, against the unchanging nature of workplaces. We might not agree with the way the world is, but we have to live in it and work in it. If we're clear about knowing the fixed from the variable we might even thrive in it.

Reality number 1

You're not really owed very much

I know. It's a bummer. Of course you *are* owed everything which is legally established, such as set wages, terms of employment or health and safety standards. At least read your contract and know your basic entitlements and rights.

You may need to know them. It's possible you could find yourself working for an employer who is less than honest.

You are owed the legally established minimum standards in most cases. You are entitled to push for the market rate if there's no 'rule'. You may not like the market rate or the industry standards but that's the current reality. Sitting around carping about the fact that cleaners earn less than stockbrokers is a waste of time. You may be right. It may be unfair, but until the market reality shifts, you are not owed much else.

You'd think you were owed basic manners and standards of decency, but that's not always a sure thing. You shouldn't feel afraid, threatened or humiliated at work, but it happens and you may not win the battle. If you have a courteous and friendly work environment, then that is a great benefit and not a **preordained right**.

There are people who are genuinely overworked and underpaid. There are people who risk their lives for others and go way beyond the call of duty. I admire them more than I can say. Unfortunately there are *also* a lot of employees who claim that they're in these groups when they clearly are not. This is why it's hard to get listened to if you say you're overworked and underpaid.

'Nothing's for nothing.' Real gains are earned or bestowed. There are few places left where promotions are automatic and if such places still exist, they are bound to be inefficient bureaucracies. (If a reward is NOT tied to performance or merit, then it is hardly a reward.)

Many benefits and conditions are just *perks*: the result of working within a certain market, for a certain kind of employer at a certain time. That is very different to a *right*. Over the years, people have told me that drink machines, a wide choice of ice cream in the canteen, promotion based on years of service, free parking spaces, delivered cups of tea, flexitime, endless sick leave and lavish Christmas dinners are amongst their *rights*. NO! They are *perks*.

I once helped to hand out bottles of good champagne in an office. Every employee got one as a 'thank you' from the company. (This was on top of an extra day's leave and three weeks' bonus pay.) I was staggered at the grunts of displeasure, the snatching of bottles and sullen comments such as 'Can't I have the cash for this?' or 'I don't like champagne!' It was a simple gesture: a nice freebie on top of very good salaries and conditions. Had those bottles been funded from my own pocket, I know I would not have bothered again.

If you are promoted or given a perk of some kind, it's probably because you earned it and/or because someone decided to give it to you. A simple thank you for a discretionary benefit would not be out of place. OK, you *have* probably earned it and it may be 'about time' but don't you like to be thanked if you do someone a favour? (Do the smart thing. A thank you would be likely to encourage more of the same.)

At least be happy about the extras and recognize a gift when you see one. Read the small print in your contract and know the difference between what you're OWED and what is GAINED.

If you want to change your money and terms, then do something *constructive* about it. If you wish to persuade and win, then be prepared with real evidence about salaries, your tangible efforts or results, and market values. Evidence might swing the case. Anger and bitching (alone) do not persuade and have the predictable result of getting other people's backs up. If reasonable attempts to get more fail, you can always 'vote with your feet' and try to find those things somewhere else.

Reality number 2

Complaining will not solve a problem

Martha from the mailroom might look as if she's listening to you. She may even be nodding in fierce agreement. But the people who might be able to DO something about your problem have probably tuned out long ago. You may be right, but no one wants to hear you.

Complaining is boring and irritating. If people are content to stand and listen to you (and many will be avoiding you), it's probably because they're waiting their turn to jump in and have a whine too.

You're wasting time (yours and other people's). You're wasting your energy. And you're probably making your situation worse because the likelihood of positive improvement has now decreased. Who wants to recruit or manage a whiner? Who wants to work near one? Who wants to help you out of it?

It takes very little talent to talk about problems. It takes talent and thought to remain professional and come up with solutions.

Whenever I bring up the subject of complaining or whining someone invariably says 'Oh, but it's fun,' which is odd because it never sounds like a barrel of laughs. I never see anyone walk away from a communal bitch session feeling better or buoyed up for action. I rarely see successful people who can spare the time for it. Complaining sucks hope and energy out of the air.

The danger is that you can become part of the problem that you're moaning about. You can be the *last* person consulted for solutions, even though you seem to have the most to say about it. You can alienate positive-minded people (who are likely to be your *most* helpful allies).

You have another option. You could be the kind of person who calms situations, listens, comes up with possibilities or ideas and inspires the people around them. And if you do find yourself getting into this awful habit of complaining, then get a bit closer to reality. Ask yourself: 'How hard is my working life?' Open a newspaper or look around. There are people with real fears and problems to contend with today.

Reality number 3

You might work with (or for) bastards

It's very likely that you will meet a lot of terrific people in your working life. You'll probably make friends for life as a consequence of working. You'll probably notice that a lot of promotions are fair or well deserved.

However, you may also meet with idle, under-qualified, unqualified or destructive people in your working life. You may come across dishonest, corrupt and unethical characters. You may find yourself working for someone with appalling manners, who shows no awareness of their behaviour and its impact on others. Should they be told about their behaviour, they may feel little or no shame.

Bullying in the workplace is a harsh reality. It's not impossible that the bully may be considered a blue-eyed boy or girl by the management. It's horrible and it isn't right, but it happens.

I once wondered whether a manager had photos of the MD with farm animals, such was the absurd level of protection afforded this dreadful man. His outrage at being caught with his hand in the till (up to his shoulder) bordered on insanity. He was allowed to take his time to find another position, in fact the chairman found a nice one for him. While the full extent of his embezzlement and greed was being investigated, a smaller petty fraud was uncovered in the same department. The junior employee was instantly dismissed and frogmarched out the door without a reference. The petty fraud was also unacceptable, but it was terrible when the younger staff decided that if you're going to be a crook, be a BIG crook. They also 'learned' that it helped if your crime embarrassed important people.

Sometimes there are people who feel they've earned the right to do as they please. Perhaps they have a connection at the top that they like to boast about. Perhaps they secured a large client or achieved some outstanding result once upon a time.

Any or all of these people may survive in their jobs. Some of them may even be promoted. They may consider themselves to be untouchable or protected by someone further up the ladder. Occasionally they *are* being protected but it is also quite possible that the significant decision makers *do not know* what's going on. Sometimes bastards are kidding themselves and surviving on borrowed time. That's IF they've been noticed and are considered to be a liability rather than an asset. They may not deserve their positions and the good fortune that goes with it. It sucks! I agree. Now what?

You always have choices about what you do. You do not have to like and love the people you work with, but you do have to be able to *work* with them. How much does this situation worry you? Is this making your life a misery? If you love what you do and want to stay, can you try to shut them out of your thoughts and get on with your day-to-day work? Do you wish to do something about this, even if the consequences (for you) are rather daunting?

Don't model yourself on these people. They may be collecting a big salary and leading the life of Riley, but you don't want to follow them. Trust me. You're better than that. Whatever you do, stay close to your own values and beliefs.

Whatever you do, stay close to your own values and beliefs.

It isn't always fair. No workplace is perfect. We may be moving closer towards true meritocracy, but it's not here yet. And this leads me to another harsh reality, which is an awkward one to describe.

Reality number 4

Your principles will be tested

You should stay close to your own values and beliefs. I mean that most sincerely, but sometimes we wobble a little.

Ideally there's a reasonable match between your values, principles and ideas and those of your employer or the clients you work for. It's never a perfect match, but ideally it's not totally fractious. Sometimes the places we work for go through change, and our beliefs and principles are challenged. (For example, I might believe in free health care but now the clinic I work for is going to charge fees.)

Sometimes the workplace changes with new owners or managers. They may have principles we either cannot fathom or are quite alien to our own. And it may not even require a large shift to get this kind of challenge. You may change position or rank to be suddenly confronted by demands that test you or situations that can try your values.

If it's a daily struggle to resolve these dilemmas and causing you considerable torment, then you might think about leaving. And that might be the right choice for you. But you may also decide to stay put and compromise.

You should take great care to avoid employers or situations that pressure you to break the law or endanger the lives of others. But there are plenty of challenges that do not constitute doing anything illegal or life-threatening.

For example, it is not always possible to be completely honest in spite of wanting to be. It is not always possible to be a caring employer or to conduct business in an open and totally scrupulous manner. The pressure to make money and survive may conflict with management's desire to hold on to staff or stay on friendly terms with those they deal with.

Try this one: if you knew that an employee had been fiddling expenses, moonlighting or extracting money from the company in some way, would you let someone know? Would you let the company know if the same person had a sick child that desperately needed expensive medical care which the family could not afford? Would your answer be affected if the directors had just granted themselves enormous bonus payments just after they'd announced a tough year and no pay rises for the rest of the staff? Not so easy, is it?

The kinds of tests and tricky situations that we can face are infinite. Whatever you choose to do, you'll learn more about yourself in the process. It is not an ideal world. Rigid unbending expectations of life and other people might not help you.

I'm not suggesting that you discard your principles. I'm just letting you know that we all can go through the mill and it's OK to talk about it. I would worry about the person who said 'Work has never presented me with a moral dilemma!'

Reality number 5

There is no job security – don't bother looking for it

The closest you might come to real job security is being good at what you do *and* getting the right people to notice it. And that's not the same thing as job security. That's being wanted or considered competent and valuable.

You are not owed a job for life. Large companies don't promise jobs for life any more, if they ever really did. They can't do it. No one knows what the workplace will be like five years from now let alone thirty years from now. Entire industries can fade away.

Restructuring, reorganizations, cutbacks, mergers, buy-outs and all the instability and radical change of the 90s have made long-term guarantees absurd. Career management is up to you. Best get used to it. There's no sign of job security returning.

Jobs for life were only a very recent phenomenon anyway. Not many of our grandparents or great-grandparents experienced such a concept. And did you ever notice the high price some people paid for having 'job security'? That kind of cushion can breed mediocrity, obedience and dependence. A 'company man' can face a slow and insidious kind of 'willpower castration' on the way through an organization. Is this what you want?

I started work in a 'safe' company that was sweeping away long-term employees. I often heard phrases like *downsizing, streamlining, culling* and *removing deadwood*. I was surrounded by much older people who had considered loyalty to be a two-way street. They were shell-shocked by their severance from a company they believed they had *served*. Most of the longer-serving staff looked up at the employer as they would look at the head of a family. (Indeed, the chairmen's portraits looked like a series of benevolent old grandfathers.) I knew that employee names had received little red crosses in meetings that were brief and perfunctory. These people had expected to retire with a gold watch and a formal gathering. They had begun to believe it was their right. They grieved over the changing world and the disappearance of the company that they once knew. Suddenly, a CV (if they even knew how to prepare one) with long years in one place and little progression, was worthless. It was as if the currency changed overnight and all their wealth was washed away. It was a salutary lesson for me. I saw it all again about ten years later in another country, and the trauma and disbelief were the same.

The reality is that you *take care of your own career* and keep your CV up to date. More importantly, *keep yourself skilled up and marketable*. New industries, professions and careers are also born. There may be great opportunities for you there. Not only is it acceptable to move around a bit, it may be the wiser thing to do. Learning different approaches and collecting new work or industry experience may be a very attractive feature on your CV.

Don't look for job security. It isn't there. Assume you could be out of a job tomorrow. (It's unlikely, however, that you would not get notice or warning.) You can do what you love and love what you do, and still keep your senses alert.

Reality number 6

No one does it alone

The truly self-made man is either a myth or an extreme rarity. Everyone has had a favour, a break or a loan from someone. Most successful people learn to ask for help and are prepared to take the risk of rejection. Most successful people have also realized that they need to attract someone's attention along the way.

There is no shame in this. If you're a very independent and self-motivated person, then you may have a problem asking for help. You may feel that favours tarnish your success. They don't. (Of course, if your success *only* rests on favours and assistance, then you're likely to be found out one day.)

Learn to ask for help. The people who can help you are not mind-readers. They don't know what you want unless you tell them. The very worst you can hear is 'sod off', and frankly, it's highly unlikely anyone will say such a thing.

Don't make your working life harder than it needs to be. A curious thing about human nature is that most people like to be asked for help (or opinions and advice) and respond very positively to a polite request.

Reality number 7

You're paid to do something – your job is not there for your benefit

Of course, you will benefit from the existence of the workplace, and that's great. But the reason the workplace is there is that someone needs it to survive and make money. (And that money ought to be more than a bank account would offer.)

In larger organizations, there's usually a shareholder seeking a return for their investment. And just like us, they would like their money to grow, or at least be secure. You might like to imagine that shareholders are 'fat cats', in pin-striped suits, smoking cigars and driving flash cars. But investors are more likely to be Wilfred and Ethel next door, pensioners or savers who might not even know where their money is invested.

Profit organizations must make a profit. They might take some losses here and there but only if they think there is a likely turnaround and gain on the way. Of course, it's fashionable to say 'We are customer focused' or 'We put people first,' and that's nice. There is no profit without customers and the united efforts of employees, but with the best will in the world, the place will go through a mighty shake-up, or even fold, if it starts bleeding money. (And that might be in spite of loyal customers and motivated staff.)

In non-profit or government organizations, there's still a customer with a need. The place may not be profit driven, but money can't be wasted either. The investor is still there, but now it's any member of the voting, tax-paying public. The organization is still expected to succeed in meeting its purpose. Workplaces that are funded by taxes are not free from observation. Increasingly, the taxpayer wants to know how their money is being spent, and rightly so.

You may work alongside people who show little interest in the REAL purpose of the organization. They may even misdirect their efforts, from wasting time and money to ignoring the customers or giving them appalling service while advising you to do the same. It can be highly confusing when the efforts of the people who run the organization (or work in it) appear to be at cross-purposes with the most basic needs of the customers and the organization. If this happens, then the organization is slowly dying, although it may not realize it yet. If the employees are directed to work in a manner that hurts the organization and its real customers then they are likely to start walking, blowing the whistle or putting their anger somewhere. Either the employee will break or the customer will uncover the hidden agenda and do something about it. We live in a consumer age. The media can train a spotlight anywhere. People can and do take their business elsewhere.

If you find a job you like, then *get very clear about the real purpose and align your efforts accordingly*. This is obvious, I know, but a large amount of bitching and wailing comes from employees who have missed this vital point. Frustration about lack of progress or reward *may* result from misguided effort and energy. Dark feelings about your work may be the result of misunderstanding the real purpose of your employment or disagreeing with it.

If you understand and agree with what your employer is trying to achieve, and you are more conscious of the kinds of actions and decisions that will enable the business to survive, then it's more likely that you will manage your time and behaviour quite differently to those who don't know or don't care about what they are working for. When you manage your time and behaviour in ways that assist the business to survive and grow, it automatically makes you more effective. The quality of being 'effective' ought to lead you to improved career prospects – at least it will in a well-run business. Smart bosses are interested in keeping and if possible, promoting effective people.

Smart bosses are interested in effective people.

Reality number 8

You cannot hide – you are responsible

If it is to be, it is up to me. If you don't like hearing that, then EEK! You could have a serious struggle in attaining real success and loving your work. You're probably not ready to make real and positive changes to your working life if you're not prepared to look at yourself.

First of all, **the main effort comes from you.** Secondly, (and here's the gritty truth) **YOU are responsible and accountable for your actions.**

Work is not beneath you. It doesn't matter who you are or where you come from (and which slave master you think you might have descended from), you are going to exert some effort. Slavery has been abolished. I know it's tempting to get some poor sod to do your photocopying and filing, and fetch you a coffee while they're at it, but alas, headcounts are getting very lean and no one wants to pay salaries for things YOU ARE BIG ENOUGH AND UGLY ENOUGH TO DO YOURSELF. It's tragic to watch the 'I've got an MBA so why should I get my own sandwich' syndrome. Tragic and hilarious!

People who protect themselves with the irrational belief that they must be right and perfect all the time are kidding themselves in the short term and setting themselves up for an enormous shock in the long term. *Yes it IS irrational!* It is simply impossible to be right and perfect all the time. It is not rational to believe that the problem is always someone else's.

No one goes out of their way to get it wrong but mistakes are a part of life. They're even a useful part of life. How else would we learn? Owning up to a mistake shows that you have integrity. (Smart employers place a high premium on integrity.)

Achievers talk about risk and loss. Successful people tend to 'recruit' colleagues who counterbalance their own strengths and weaknesses. That requires at least three skills. The first is astute self-awareness. You really have to know your strengths and weaknesses. The second is the capacity to listen to, and make good use of, other people's contributions. The third skill is to know how to find and keep such people.

And finally, in spite of the obsession in the 80s and 90s with blaming others and sidestepping personal accountability, the psychologically healthy person stays in tune with reality. And the reality is, we just cannot go on shoving blame at others for the things we have done.

If I have burned my finger on a perfectly good toaster, then that is my stupid fault. Similarly, if I trip on a paving stone, then that is also my stupid fault for not watching where I was going. If you make a mistake at work, do something about it. Say 'sorry' at least. Don't look for someone else to blame. Don't hide the problem, lie about it or run away from it. If you make a decision, accept the consequences. Great human beings tend to do this. If you wish to succeed, then accept responsibility and behave with dignity. It's the weasel who says 'It's not my problem' when it clearly is.

Don't be an emotional bonsai! You're wonderful and fabulous, but you're not perfect. We all have strengths and weaknesses. Every weakness can be endearing. Any strength can be overdone to the point where it becomes a weakness.

CHAPTER 3

HOW TO BE EFFECTIVE, SUCCESSFUL AND VALUED AT WORK

get what you want without hurting people or losing your integrity

"As one goes through life one learns that if you don't paddle your own canoe, you don't move."

Katherine Hepburn

If you want to love your work, then a breakthrough could start with a change in your attitudes. There are two attitudes that might need a bit of an overhaul. One is your attitude to yourself, and the other is your attitude to work itself. *You* are the greatest ally or hindrance to having a working life that is enjoyed rather than endured.

We are valued for our attitude to work

An important, but largely secret, rule of work is that we are employed for our skills (or potential to develop a skill), but we are valued for our attitude. Unfortunately very few people will ever tell you exactly what they mean by the 'right' or 'wrong' attitude and how that translates to workday behaviour.

There are no absolute rules to follow. I know how I feel about work but I can't tell you it's the right way. It's not a right and wrong kind of subject. There's no 'right' career path to follow.

Whatever your goals or ambitions (and you don't have to be ruthlessly ambitious with a desire to rule the world) your attitude to work, or work ethic, will influence the way you commit yourself to the job and the way you relate to other

The better your attitude to work, the more likely you are to be successful.

people. This in turn will impact your ability to find and keep work that feels right for you.

The better your attitude to work, the more likely you are to be successful – and enjoy what you do. I believe that this holds the key to loving what you do for a living.

Now, I'm not saying here that if you follow the advice below, it gives a cast-iron guarantee of a meteoric rise through the company and universal adoration. It's just like your health – you can stay fit and eat well and still get sick. You can do all the right things and still be at the receiving end of unfair decisions or find that you just don't fit in. And no one is ever admired and loved by all. What I am saying, however, is that this is what will dramatically increase your chances for a successful and fulfilling working life.

So what would the perfect attitude look like in practice? In other words, how do managers want their team to behave? What do they want to see them do? And how?

The following advice is based on a survey of highly effective managers, asking them to specify exactly what they long to see in their ideal employee. I've distilled their wants and needs into a code for success:

1. How to react to the work that is given to you:
   - Deliver the quality requested
   - Deliver on time
   - Do what is asked for, once the opportunity for questions and concerns has passed
   - Tell your manager of any problem affecting a deadline or delivery (Give them feedback on progress or problems)
   - Seek clarification, but not for the same things over and over again
   - Do more than your manager asks for, but don't go off on a tangent

- Get the things you need for the work, using your own initiative
- Take some pride in your work
- Focus on the success of the task
- Put quality as a priority, if it is deemed to be one
- Say 'We can do this.' Have some idea as to 'how', and that 'how' should not include lots of shouting
- Do what is required, but add a bit of style to it
- Follow the task through to the end without fuss
- Refrain from complaining and moaning
- Hear the dimensions and constraints of the task before reacting

2. How to behave and use your time:

- Behave in a way that assists, rather than disrupts, completion
- Maintain a sense of balance between being human and getting on with the job
- Stay when the pressure is on – go home when it's off
- Put in the *full day,* as determined by the culture or terms
- Don't fake sick leave or treat it as leave entitlement
- Keep to the expected contract
- Keep personal phone calls to a reasonable length and frequency
- Work extra time (within reason) without expecting payment, because you're interested
- Be proactive rather than reactive (Don't sit and wait for the next task. Let them know you've finished, rather than wait to be 'caught' free of work.)

- Volunteer without having to be 'press-ganged'
- Show up on time to work and meetings

3. What to show in terms of character traits:

- Enthusiasm
- Dependability
- Honour (you can be trusted with money and property)
- Flexibility (you show a willingness to modify a work method or behaviour for the sake of the bigger task without being aggressive or defensive)
- The ability to criticize constructively
- Accountability and responsibility (you don't blame, find excuses or use smokescreens)
- Healthy scepticism and humour (you're able to laugh at the work and the workplace, but get on with it anyway)
- The capacity to admit a mistake or be wrong
- A generally upbeat, friendly and optimistic manner
- A sense of humour that falls short of whoopee cushions and furniture dismantling
- Confidence without arrogance
- A positive attitude – but not a suicidal optimism
- Honesty that is not tactless or cruel
- Individuality (you are not a follower of the mob; you're able to think independently)
- The ability to express your feelings (with good manners) about the 'reasonableness' of the workload
- Ambition (without being too obvious about it)

4. Thinking or mental attributes:

- Be prepared to cope with change
- Have a 'continuous learning' philosophy
- Be realistic without being too constrained by reality (We need dreamers too!)
- Be interested in the wider issues
- Show an interest in the business, market or industry
- Learn quickly (at least fast enough to grasp a situation or learn a skill that is required)
- Make decisions with an eye on the time constraints
- Know and understand how your work fits in
- Know and understand where the work of others impacts the task
- Be willing to question the status quo (Employers do want people who think there must be better ways to do things)
- Have a childlike curiosity
- Be 'willing' rather than 'expert'
- Don't expect to always have the answer (be prepared to discuss a problem)

5. Ways to interact with others that you work with

- Open and honest disagreement without aggression
- Courtesy and good manners
- Avoidance of most office politics and corridor gossip
- Clear communication and openness (no 'knowledge is power' behaviour)
- Co-operative behaviour (don't start conflicts)

- Consideration for all those people impacted by the work
- Sincere (but not intrusive) concern for the welfare of your colleagues
- Good listening
- Charm and equanimity in behaviour, especially in front of customers and clients
- Offer suggestions
- Give credit and admit mistakes
- Acceptance of people as they are (without prejudice)
- Cleanliness (bathe often, at least with consideration for other people)
- Seek other people's assistance, opinions, advice or help
- Take your turn to make tea or coffee or buy the round and even, taking on team leadership when the need arises.

No one is expected to do ALL of these things ALL of the time. No one is expected to be perfect. (That would be too weird!) But within these responses, you can see patterns of behaviour that indicate a positive or healthy work attitude from a manager's point of view.

Not one of the managers I surveyed mentioned obedience, devotion, forsaking an outside life, working to the point of exhaustion, silence, speaking only when spoken to, wearing their Sunday best, expertise in all things, a high IQ or being ecstatically happy all the time.

I only listed the word *enthusiasm* once (under character traits) but it came up many times. This does not imply being bug-eyed on adrenalin. Enthusiasm does not mean grinning from ear to ear all day. It means 'upbeat', with humour, optimism and interest.

It's hard to separate enthusiasm from a healthy work attitude. Do we enjoy a task (and show enthusiasm) because we do it well, or do we do it well because we enjoy it and have enthusiasm for it? Whatever the answer, rewards are more likely to come to those who do it well.

"Bad employers will not care whether you enjoy a particular task. . . . they will only want to know if you know how to do it. But good employers will care greatly. They know that unless a would-be employee has enthusiasm for his or her work, the quality of that work will always suffer."

Richard Nelson Bolles, author, What Color Is Your Parachute?

Your attitude is going to influence your behaviour, and it's your behaviour that others respond to. People will make assumptions about your attitude from observing the things you say and do.

Other people's happiness and safety can be impacted by our attitude. When we do not give a damn (at one extreme) or become so driven that we are exhausted, *we* impact on *other* people.

It's not only your attitude that can impact on other people. There is also a range of behaviours, habits and mannerisms that can really undermine your chances of being valued and successful.

Consider the feedback nobody wants to tell you

You might wonder how this can make any sense. How can you consider it feedback if you never hear it? But here's the awkward question: *have you been passed over for promotion too many times?* Do you seem to be overly competent in your field but people who joined years after you have now moved on to better things? How did you get left behind? If you didn't choose to stay behind, it could be that you are not considered promotable for some reason that you're not aware of.

Habits and hygiene

Has a bar of soap ever been left on your desk? Do people make excuses to avoid standing too close? Body odour has to be at the top of the list of unspeakable feedback items, narrowly followed by atrocious table manners, appalling/ inappropriate dress standards, bad breath, dandruff and weeping sores.

Those who might promote you are also shy of talking to you about habits like fiddling, picking, scratching, and nose mining that cause a range of reactions from amusement to distress from others.

You may think I'm kidding but I have had this conversation with many managers and their concern is over hurting feelings and not knowing what to say. Their reluctance to promote is to do with the reactions of customers and clients – usually. (If it's only the staff in Accounts who are fainting, they might think this is a tolerable price to pay.)

The fine line

You should also consider what is considered acceptable in terms of drink and drugs usage and whether you can be trusted to stay in control. You may be the office hero for some of your dangerous, school-kid-like practical jokes and the 'funny stories' about how you wind up on the floor at social events, but it is not likely to impress good managers looking to develop others. More and more employers are heading down the zero tolerance line on drink and drugs. There are so many mixed messages about alcohol that it can be easy to misunderstand the 'rules'.

Use some common sense and remember you're at work whether it's a lunch with wine on the table, the office picnic or the Christmas party. From finding your photocopied private parts on the notice boards to having to apologize to the boss for saying her kids looked like monkeys, drink can still cause your ruin.

What not to do

Also under the heading of problems that are muttered about but rarely tackled properly come the following habits that can land you in the dead-end file.

These include:

- following the crowd at every opportunity
- watching the clock every single day
- thriving on gossip

- being fabulously indiscreet and unable to keep anything in confidence
- fiddling expenses or constantly stretching it a bit
- grabbing what you can, whenever you can – but just falling short of theft
- championship belligerence

Belligerent employees irritate co-workers and managers by overusing phrases such as 'no' or 'not my job' or 'do I have to' or 'why should I' or 'I'll do it – in my time' every single time they're asked to do something. (You might think it's funny. It's a rare manager who agrees with you.)

None of these things will probably get you fired. Rarely would they earn you a warning, but they will also be used as a valid reason for holding you back from positions of responsibility. And to repeat the point, it's highly likely that no one will ever tell you why you're not getting any-where in a hurry.

How to become promotable without losing integrity

My ex-colleague, Tim, decided to be proactive (no bad thing) and requested a private talk with his manager. With good manners, he tried to negotiate a rise, explaining that unless his salary improved 'he'd have to start looking around for something else'. His manager smiled kindly and said 'OK.' And that was the end of their conversation.

Tim is a very nice man with an apparently healthy self-esteem. He works the hours he is supposed to and gets along with people. He's capable of doing the work he is paid to do and produces the results he's asked for. He does not create problems for the company. And the manager is also a very nice man. He's smart, very focused and runs his part of the business effectively.

Tim is still in the same job. He's quite unhappy now. He thinks that his manager doesn't particularly care whether he comes or goes. He doesn't really know why he didn't get a rise. He hasn't asked for feedback. Tim now claims that he's 'trapped'. He assumes he's supposed to try harder but doesn't know if he can work longer hours or put in more sweat than he already does.

But it may not be about trying harder. It's far more likely that you'll love your work if it brings you the rewards you seek. To negotiate for the things you want, you need to have some power to your elbow. You have to be someone who is valued.

Unfortunately, Tim isn't deemed to be extraordinary in any way. He's useful, certainly. But in the current market, he's also highly replaceable. It's not that the manager wants him to go, but he's not going to any lengths to persuade Tim to stay.

How to become highly valued

In case you're already humming 'The Impossible Dream', fear not! The following ten qualities are not inborn. Tim (and anyone else) can learn and improve on all or some of these areas. Keep working at this stuff, and it's far more likely that managers will try to keep you – with promotion, transfer, assisted further education, more interesting work, flexible hours, pay rises, perks – whatever you seek. If you want to daydream in peace, they might even clear the space for you to do that. In other words, it's far *more likely* that you will get into a strong bargaining position in any negotiation with your employer(s) if you can develop these qualities.

But to be fair, I must warn you that you may encounter people who do NONE of these useful things and yet have risen up through an organization. Life is not always fair.

And following these top ten is not a guarantee of job security. You may do all of these things expertly and still be out of a job, *but it is far less likely*. Even if it does happen, you won't be unemployed for long.

1. Value time.

Value your own time, as well as the time of others. Time deserves to be valued because it is the stuff that life is made of. Fritter away time and you waste life.

Time is not against you. Nothing could be fairer than time. Every single person is allotted 24 hours in a day. What separates us is the way we use our time and manage our own behaviour.

There is no such thing as 'time management'. Time cannot be managed or controlled. Time rolls on regardless of anything you do. Time is not the problem and gadgets are not the answer. *Self-awareness* and a *keen sense of purpose* are more important than any diary, electronic organizer, e-mail, voice mail or call blocking system.

How do you get a keener sense of purpose? Stay very close to this question: 'What are the really important things that I must do to make a success of this job?' The answer will often boil down to two or three particular things. If you don't know what those things are, someone else will. Try asking the boss, the boss's boss or a valued customer if you don't know where to start. Someone must know. (If nobody has a clue, then leave. The job is going nowhere).

When you know the answer, keep it with you and use it as a compass. You now have direction. You will get distractions, but you have the means to get back on track. You won't get to your success or key results in a straight line. Life isn't like that.

Most of your energy must then be applied towards things that have a direct connection with the answer. A lot of requests and tasks that come your way will not be connected. Learn to prioritize and choose. Not everything is important. Not everything is urgent.

By the way, it's a rare individual that admits to wasting time. Typically, people imagine that time-wasting would be obvious and possibly resemble staring out the window or counting up paper clips. But plenty of people do expend energy on things that are not important. Time-wasters can look terribly active and exhaust themselves within the day. Time-wasters can become indignant at the very idea that they might be inefficient. 'Me? Waste time? I work very hard you know!'

Combine a keen sense of direction with a reasonable amount of flexibility. What are you going to do? Refuse to stop and sing 'Happy Birthday' to a colleague because it's not one of your priorities? Learn to be 'ruthless with time and gracious with people'.

Learn to value the time spent in planning and thinking. Would you let someone build you a house without a plan? Do you think you'll be a valued employee if you cannot plan or appreciate its value?

Working *hard* is not always the right thing to do. It's not necessarily valued. Filling out a time sheet with lots of hours on it does *not* necessarily mean that you are held in high regard. Tim always *did the things he was asked to do*. That's always better than an obstructive or awkward employee, but it does not necessarily spell 'star' to an employer.

2. Value energy

This is closely related to the use of time, but deserves its own space.

Learn to value your own mental and physical energy as a resource that can be purposefully directed or wasted. The road to hell is paved with good intentions. So is the road to working day misery, tiredness and distress. Working hard, showing up on time and doing as you're told are fine, but it's not enough to make you a highly valued employee.

Looking busy without questioning the importance of the task is not terribly clever. Business does not depend on 'busyness'. Smart employers don't confuse activity with results. Their priority is the *result* and the *quality of the result.*

Smart employers want *effective* people. It's nice to be efficient and do things right but it's MORE important to be effective and do the right job. Efficiency without effectiveness can make you a hard-working waster of energy.

Smart businesses love people who find clever shortcuts – ways of saving time and energy without compromising the result or creating more problems in the long run.

Smart employers want *effective* people. Respect other people's energy. Pushing work deemed as 'unimportant' on to others is not a solution. (And if you like the buzz of working late hours for the sake of it – that's great. It doesn't mean other people have to join you. They may have better things to do.)

Everyone needs to recharge. Everyone needs a life away from work. We cannot work anywhere near our peak if we are tired. However, a certain amount of pressure and stress is necessary. Too little can lead us to feel lethargic or bored. Too much and we're liable to snap under the strain.

"Every now and then go away, have a little relaxation, for when you come back to your work your judgement will be surer since to remain constantly at work will cause you to lose the power of judgement"

Leonardo Da Vinci

As a harder lesson to learn, value energy as a way of respecting your own health and that of others. It's unlikely you'll be able to love your work if it's making you ill.

3. Respect others and earn it in return

Nobody successfully *demands* respect. It is not a right. It does *not* automatically flow from the possession of a title. Respect has to be earned It is usually earned because it is given out. Respect is not an automatic belief in someone else's superiority. Respect is about showing consideration.

To earn respect, other people must believe that you think *before* you speak. They must believe you are stable and have control over your own behaviour. Listening, staying calm and keeping a cool head are great respect earners. Unpredictable behaviour usually spells 'unprofessional'.

If you want to release some anger, then save it for a choice occasion. Direct your anger, if you must, at an important issue, rather than at a person or group. Make this a rare event, and people will probably believe that this issue is important to you. Lose your temper on a regular basis and you become the office entertainment. People with a short fuse have to become louder, sillier and more animated to make a point because others become desensitized to their noise.

Find the very short amount of time it takes to acknowledge people and be pleasant. Everyone deserves basic courtesy and consideration. Other people have needs, hopes, dreams, lives and a right to be themselves.

A wise person shows *sincere* respect for other people's contributions. All kinds of skills are needed. All manner of contributions make a success. Recognize your own strengths and limitations. Know that you can benefit from the strengths of others.

"No one is useless in this world who lightens the burdens of another."

Charles Dickens

You may be very smart. It is not enough. You may feel that you have good connections. That's not a genuine respect earner. Giving respect is the only known way of getting it back in return.

4. Think and choose

"A great many people think they are thinking when they are merely rearranging their prejudices."

William James

The ability to question and think is not a gift that only a few lucky people are born with. Anyone can develop thinking skills. If you struggle with thinking skills, there are many guides and techniques around to help you learn. But this is all dependent upon your willingness to be open to this kind of learning.

Some people are reluctant to spend time thinking because they are afraid that it doesn't look busy. Thinking usually requires listening, concentrating and a bit of quiet. You cannot do this if you only want to be seen to be busy and hear the sound of your own voice.

The desire to rush in and ACT, DO or SOLVE is very powerful. But the question 'How will I do this' is as valid as the question 'What will I do?' Know that you have choices, and use the moments between every stimulus and response to THINK.

A business that is searching for valuable employees is not really interested in people who are good at memorizing. They don't need more yes men. (There are plenty of those). They don't need as many pairs of hands.

Businesses needs more thinkers, creators, innovators, problem solvers, decision makers and responsibility takers. Businesses need people who **can** and **will** ask smart questions (and preferably get involved in the solutions).

No matter how far technology advances, machinery is unlikely to replace a truly agile brain in our lifetime.

"One machine can do the work of fifty ordinary men. No machine can do the work of one extraordinary man."

E Hubbard

5. Be brave

Brave does not mean fearless. Only a truly stupid person could be without fear. Fear keeps us alive. Courage is the *mastery* of fear.

In the workplace, complacency and laziness are greater enemies of bravery than cowardice. Good enough *IS* sometimes good enough. A customer does not always seek the highest quality. But it is not good enough to be miserable at work, to deliberately underachieve or complain because you expect someone else to fix up your life for you.

"We become just by performing just actions, temperate by performing temperate actions, brave by performing brave actions."

Aristotle

Be brave enough to stand apart from the crowd and hear their laughter or anger. Be brave enough to seek honest feedback in order to grow. Confront issues or problems and see them through to a solution. Be brave enough to take a calculated risk.

We show bravery by giving encouragement to others. When we step away from the insecure desire to compete with or stifle those around us, we are braver.

We show bravery by taking responsibility. The world of business is desperately short of people who will say 'This is what I stand for, here is what I promise to do and I will see it through. I will fix things if there is a problem.' This kind of behaviour is very rare in sick organizations. Employers looking to survive and grow will search for it and reward it.

Success takes risk, sweat, frustration, effort and bravery. It is pursued without guarantees and brave people know this.

6. Judge the line between persisting and giving up

"Nothing in the world can take the place of persistence. Talent will not; nothing is more common than unsuccessful men with talent. Genius will not; unrewarded genius is almost a proverb. Education alone will not; the world is full of educated derelicts. Persistence and determination alone are omnipotent."

Calvin Coolidge

The quality of persistence is intertwined with bravery and energy.

I can't help noticing that the smartest people do not necessarily make the grade. Nor do the incredibly brilliant always cope very well with life at work. Qualifications from the right places still attract attention and often result in a better start in a career, but that's usually it. The quality that continues to divide people, whatever the fashion for winners or 'stars', is the ability to persist. Put simply – it is the ability to *get back up* and try again.

Without persistence, it's hard to face the down times, the slow times, the boredom, the criticism, the refusals, the rejections and all the obstacles that block our paths from time to time. Without persistence, we may not be finishers or achievers.

Children can be shamelessly persistent. They can ask for the same thing twenty times, knowing very well that the power of persistence is likely to make us cave in. They're not embarrassed to hear a loud 'NO'. They do not run away at the first refusal. As adults, we learn to respect another person's NO (or at least we should) but this learning can too easily become a habit of giving up on things that *could* be pursued.

Perhaps the highly creative types, who are sometimes accused of remaining in a 'childlike' state, also have something to teach us.

The Beatles were rejected from one record company with the feedback, 'We don't like their sound. Guitar music is on the way out.' Elvis Presley was fired after one performance with the helpful advice, 'You ain't goin' nowhere, son. You ought to go back to drivin' a truck.' A 'talent scout' said of Fred Astaire, 'Can't act, can't sing. Slightly bald. Can dance a little.'

There is a line *at work* between pursuing your talents and dreams in spite of rejection and changing tack when you need to. Pursuing a work or business goal is not exactly the same as the persistence behind a creative or inventive talent. At work, we have to consider other people's money and the risks THEY would wish us to take with it. We probably have customers to consider and other employees whose lives are affected by our risks.

No one can tell you where the line is, and there are examples of success in persistence beyond all good sense. Drawing the line (at work) will depend on your ability to look things in the eye and listen carefully. Another person's squawk of disapproval may be a genuine sign that you've gone too far *or* their very timid reaction to any kind of risk taking.

Be willing to say, 'YES. We can do it. It can be done. Let's go back and try again.' But also learn the language of 'NO. This is wrong. This isn't working. This cannot be done. Let's change tack. I made a mistake. Let's think again.'

7. Continue to develop self-awareness

"Men stumble over the truth from time to time, but most pick themselves up and hurry off as if nothing happened."

Churchill

Given feedback that describes our poor behaviour, we can shrug it off, attack the person who gave it (sometimes called 'shooting the messenger'), talk about our good intentions or justify ourselves in some way.

Seek feedback. Be brave enough to hear it and take action even though you know it's filtered and skewed by human perception. Practise the things you need to work on with the genuine aim of improvement. Constructive feedback can flow easily where people feel a genuine sense of openness and a respect for honesty.

Skilful people often appear to be 'naturals' and maintain standards that we might find intimidating. Ask them how they got that way, and they're likely to confess that their 'gift' is a habit they have learned and developed.

You also need to hear about the things you're doing well and the things that people *appreciate* about you. Not just for the warm glow that this provides, but so that you don't stop doing the good things. It's a funny thing. Some people are afraid to hear the worst, while some fear discovering their personal best.

Without feedback, how will you know if you're valued? How will you know if you're achieving the results? How will you know where and how to improve? How will you head off a problem before it becomes a crisis? (Tim had a wonderful opportunity to seek some feedback, but slunk away instead.)

Clinging to little work tribes with only those you 'like' is limiting. Get out and talk to people. Seek mentors, sponsors, constructive critics and a wider variety of opinions and ideas.

8. Get a little more comfortable with change

"When James Watt invented that steam engine, thousands of ten-year-old boys who had been hauling coal carts were put out of work. However, this left them free to do other things, such as live to be eleven."

P J O'Rourke

People can fear and resist change without always seeing the opportunities and improvements it can bring. Change can displace jobs but that is often quite a slow process and it's usually predictable. Where change displaces work, the same technology often creates new opportunities. When work closes down in one location, it invariably moves to others.

It's natural for people to feel touchy about change. We like consistency. We fear the unknown. We like our habits or we wouldn't have them.

Workplaces that never change are committed to their own demise. So we must get used to change, but not all changes in the workplace are smart or advantageous. Accepting that a change has occurred or *will be made* is wise. Acceptance does *not* mean agreement. It means 'coming to terms with a change'. At the end of acceptance you may decide to go. You're free to say, 'I accept this change has happened but it's not for me.'

You have choices. Speak up or be silent. Stay or move. Wishing for the change to reverse, or just go away, is a waste of time. Pretending the change has not occurred is called 'denial'. Trying to undermine the change or make sure it doesn't stand a chance of success is called 'sabotage'. Denial and sabotage are not going to lead you back to feeling good about yourself and your work.

Asking questions, getting information and finding out what the change will mean is called 'exploration' and it's the faster road to getting back on track.

"When one door closes, another opens; but we often look so long and so regretfully upon the closed door that we do not see the one which has opened for us. "

Alexander Graham Bell

Valued employees are also at ease with the idea that they may need to make a change in their *own* behaviour. Be willing to look at your own habits or inflexible beliefs that may be causing your unhappiness.

9. Be more than willing and able.

But at least **be willing and able**! Nobody is absolutely indispensable, but some employees are easier to say good-bye to.

A smart business hates to lose its valued people but doesn't mind trimming off the deadwood. Given free choice, that is usually where the axe falls first. What is **deadwood**? It's an awful term, but it's a familiar one to any manager who ever made cutbacks.

Deadwood refers to those employees who have ceased to grow and develop with the workplace. Their contributions are marginal. They are not considered to be necessary for future survival and growth. In fact, the removal of dead-wood may be considered a good thing to HELP the business survive and grow.

Businesses need a variety of people from 'big picture thinkers' to precise, detailed 'expert' types to dependable 'doing' types. In good times and bad, a smart business will keep revisiting these questions 'What is it that we do?' and 'What are the results we seek?' Then there will be a focus on those employees whose results make up the answer.

When the 'deadwood' are asked to leave, there are protests about losing loyal people. But don't confuse loyalty with long service. The two things may or may not be related.

Those who are very hard to replace, who bring in work, who attract other talented staff, who can inspire and get the best from others, who can think, choose and make timely decisions, these people are the 'stud stock' of a business. It's a blow to a business when they are lost. It is NOT a bad thing to lose the deadwood.

10. Keep a sense of humour and perspective

"Work is much more fun than fun."

Noel Coward

But sometimes you need to remind yourself to laugh.

There is no particular task or set of work conditions that carries the 'secret' of happiness at work. There is a great deal of fun to be had from the work itself, the disciplines imposed, the company of other human beings and from the knowledge that we are employed and making a contribution. (Try a spell of unemployment if you doubt it.) In every kind of work, there is the opportunity for learning, fun and a sense of achievement.

CHAPTER 4

THE POWER OF YOUR BELIEFS

how success and defeat
may lie within

"Not in the clamour of the crowded street, not in the shouts and plaudits of the throng, but in ourselves are triumph and defeat."

Henry Wadsworth Longfellow

There are strong links between your self-image and your confidence levels, aspirations and general optimism. That's probably not much of a surprise. The more you believe you have lots of positive qualities, are good at what you do and have a lot going for you, then the more confident and optimistic you are likely to be. What you believe about yourself is very powerful.

It's all too easy to assume that this means that intelligent people in prestigious jobs have a high self-image and those less academically inclined in less glamorous work have a lower self-image. Not true. Street sweepers may love their work and be happy while lawyers may have deep feelings of dissatisfaction and self-loathing. Don't make the mistake of assuming that a low self-image only applies to the chronically unemployed or less desirable (to you) kinds of work.

Underachievers may be happy with their lot – then again – they *may* be underachieving because they are too afraid to take risks or try new things because of a prevailing fear of failure. This low self-image may mean that low-achievers have a destructive habit of talking themselves into settling for less. An example might be an assistant who doesn't apply for the next job up because they don't believe they could do the job (when everybody else thinks they'd be fine). They are being limited by their beliefs.

Overachievers *may* also have a low self-image, if 'never good enough' feelings dominate their working lives. Overachievers might feel that unless they over-accumulate, constantly climb the ladder, show symbolic evidence of their success and score points, then they're not acceptable. (That is *not* unconditional positive regard.) There might also be constant self-doubt, an inability to share the credit, an inability to relax, take risks or make decisions. Mistakes become a personal issue, rather than a learning point or the necessary price of experimenting. 'NO GOOD' and 'NEVER GOOD ENOUGH' are the neon signs that flash for 24 hours in the mind of someone with a low self-image. Their happiness is being limited by their beliefs – and possibly their career too.

Your self-image impacts your search for work, your expectations, comfort with what you're doing and your acceptance of the work situation. An unhealthy or distorted self-image can lead to a confused sense of your abilities and unrealistically high or low expectations. It has an impact on the extreme ends of achievement – *you can't observe someone's self-image by simply looking at their career choices and pay cheques.*

How does our self-image affect our lives?

Not only do your beliefs about yourself (your self-image) affect your own confidence and optimism, they also communicate a very strong message about you to other people.

Imagine you're driving and need to stop for petrol, food and a break. You'll probably hope for good service. You expect the pumps to be working. You hope to eat good, safe food. You want a pleasant, trouble-free stop. It's not an unreasonable expectation.

On one side of the road there are a series of signs for a petrol stop coming up. They read: 'Running low on petrol. Our food is pretty awful. Why would you want to stop here? We're OK, I suppose but we're thinking of closing down. Might as well! What's the point?'

On the other side of the road, another petrol station advertises like this: 'We're open! Can we help you? Friendly service! We serve great breakfasts! Best coffee for miles! Give yourself a break and stop in for a while!'

Where do you want to stop? A rational person will choose the place that *seems* confident and capable, the one that seems helpful, effective and upbeat. A sensible person tries to save time and energy and prefers to be amongst pleasant, welcoming people.

Why would you be interested in stopping, except out of pity or curiosity, at the first place? You would stop there ONLY IF YOU HAD NO CHOICE. (And you would expect problems, so you would not be in the best mood as you pulled up.)

We are, not very surprisingly, quite interested in our own needs and wants. In our lives, we're not unlike the motorist searching about for service. We react in similar ways when we're given a choice between dealing with someone who exhibits hopelessness and someone who displays confidence.

It's sad that a lot of people start out with a low opinion of themselves, but in the workplace, it's human and predictable that managers would rather not rely on such people. Unless we are very kind people and interested in helping others to lift up their lives and reach their potential, we will gravitate towards more optimistic, upbeat human beings when we want something.

Put yourself in the shoes of an employer. Any business is trying to survive, profit and meet its demands. Businesses want confident, upbeat people when they recruit and promote. Employers want people with the independent will to act and make decisions, solve problems, attract customers or just understand the purpose of the organization and put their effort into achieving it. They rarely have the time to build the confidence of employees and prove to someone with a chronically low self-image that they are OK. Few businesses have the skill to do it in any case.

Sometimes a business can help to build self-esteem because positive experiences, like being trusted and having some feedback about achievement and success, help to build a positive self-image. (But that's a happy accident.)

All kinds of people find employment. Someone with a *chronically* low self-image can still get a job because an employer cannot afford the confident, happy and optimistic people that it really wants. But you aren't going to progress very far or get the best work given to you if you're sending out the wrong messages.

Where does self-image come from?

If you want to love your work, then you'll never have a greater enemy or ally than the voice in your own head. The capacity of your own self-image to help or hinder you goes ahead of natural talents and abilities, opportunities and qualifications.

"When young, [circus elephants] are attached by heavy chains to large stakes driven deep into the ground. They pull and yank and strain and struggle, the chain is too strong, the stake too rooted. One day they give up, having learned that they cannot pull free, and from that day forward they can be 'chained' with a slender rope. When this enormous animal feels any resistance, though it has the strength to pull the whole circus tent over, it stops trying. Because it believes it cannot – it cannot."

Gavin de Becker

Some people put success and happiness down to luck. Some put success down to being in the right place at the right time, but if you don't believe in yourself, you're unlikely to grasp any opportunity that arises if you're convinced you'll only mess it up anyway. Some people put success and happiness down to talent and ability, but what makes us persist with our skills and learning if it's not the inner belief that we can improve and develop?

If you don't believe you can succeed, you are unlikely to start the journey toward a goal. How can we pursue anything at all if we believe ourselves to be unworthy? The elephant does not bother to pull the chain because it believes it cannot be free. And too many people will scoff at the idea of loving their work because they don't believe it is possible for them. The facts and realities of their careers, job markets and employment situations are as irrelevant as the strength of that chain to the elephant.

If you don't have a high enough self-image, you may give up or give in at the first moment of criticism or rejection since you've had 'proof' that the outside world agrees with your estimation of yourself. You need, at a minimum, some faith in your own abilities and a strong enough feeling of self-worth. 'Strong enough' means *enough* to overcome disappointment, failure and destructive criticism. You need a self-image that is strong enough to *accept yourself* and take *a sense of pride* in what you're pursuing and doing.

Our 'helpful' subconscious mind stores everything as fact. In the storage compartment, there is no judgement. Information is taken in on good faith, whether it's right or wrong, destructive or helpful. This also means that *the messages we take in about ourselves from other people are all stored as fact* in the subconscious mind.

By the time we reach seven or eight years of age we may have a fairly consistent answer to the question 'What kind of person am I?' Whenever you start a sentence with 'I am' or 'I'm the kind of person who . . .' or 'That's just not me' or 'I can (or I cannot) see myself being . . .' you are taking your cue from the self-image 'file' you have stored in your subconscious mind. If you pause to answer the question 'Who do you think you are?', you are taking a moment to get the file out and have a look. When you're asked about your potential, strengths, weaknesses and capacities, you're being asked to refer to that file. Those are the obvious moments in which we think about or refer to our self-image. There are also many moments when the referral is not so obvious.

We refer to our subconscious mind before we do, say or feel anything. So its influence on our working lives is extreme and constant. It guides the choices we make, the aspirations we hold on to, the ways in which we strive or risk, the ways in which we listen to people and carry out tasks. Our self-image helps to guide our pen as we compile a report or pitch an idea. It guides the way in which we talk to our colleagues and just about every single thing we do, from the time we show up to the way we take care of the tools we're given.

What could happen if we started out in life hearing too many put-downs? Our self-image not only *impacts*, it even *directs* our behaviour. And then our behaviour impacts the way that other people react to us. Therefore, our self-image affects the kind of life we are going to lead. It also impacts and directs the working lives we lead. People can only respond to (reward, punish or ignore) our behaviour. They cannot read our thoughts. As yet, we cannot see true potential and intelligence in another person. We can only make assumptions based upon their behaviour.

There's a possibility here for a **cycle of self-destruction or happiness**. It seems very unfair that other people may heap 'reinforcement' on top of a low self-image, but such is life. As Marcus Aurelius noticed long ago, 'Our life is what our thoughts make of it.'

The low self-image trap

If I start out with low confidence and the expectation of failure, I will probably experience feelings of hopelessness, anxiety and tension. I'm not likely to be very creative since creativity relies on playful risk. A mistake is confirmation of my hopelessness. I do not perform at my best. Criticism or failure confirms the 'fact' that I am hopeless and incapable. A self-fulfilling, self-destructive process begins because I engage in self-talk and try to convince myself that my original belief was the right one. (Have you ever tried to say something nice to someone with very low self-confidence and then felt that your compliment was being thrown back at you?)

It's the most frustrating part of the low self-image trap that we *can* (and often do) continue the self-destructive cycle ourselves. No matter who gave us the negative message first time around, it is **our own self-talk that can continue to replay and re-record the damage**.

So how are you feeling right now?

I notice that few people have led an insult-free life. Talking about the self-image stirs people. We remember those who gave us feelings of self-worth and encouraged us to reach for something. (We remember the other voices too!) Talking about the self-image can bring many emotions to the surface. It's a sensitive subject.

We don't have to share personal information or describe our self-image for work purposes. (Just as well!) It is not appropriate to start questioning others about their self-image or to dig into personal archives that people wish to keep private. It isn't necessary to stop and navel gaze all day, forever questioning your self-image.

But let's be clear – you cannot separate work performance from this concept. If people become more aware and thoughtful of how their words and insults and compliments land on others, then that is no bad thing. Indeed, for managers it is a critical part of professional development.

What else can be done?

Can we use the delete button on the more hurtful parts of our self-image – the bits that others inputted that we recognize as damaging or limiting in some way? Dr Denis Waitley writes that 'billions of integrated and separate items of input over a lifetime are all there awaiting retrieval. They can never be wilfully erased by you. You can override them with stronger messages or modify their effects over a period of time, but you own them for life.'

It's lucky for us that self-talk exists. Self-talk goes on in the conscious mind where there is the capacity to weigh things up. Our conscious mind CAN judge information about the present moment. Our conscious mind CAN make decisions and choices today if we seize the moment of choice before we react.

YOU CAN catch yourself hearing the negative voices that spew up from your memory and accompany a low self-image and **MODIFY** the effects over time. (You can tell your self-talk to shut up!)

You cannot go back and ask every single person to change their opinion and take back their comments. You need to look ahead now.

YOU CAN discredit the opinion of others. People under stress, those lacking in communication skills, brilliant perception or understanding of potential damage, may not have acted out of malice. That's not an excuse for hurtful words and actions, but we can stand back and ask 'Well, what did THEY know?'

You cannot erase the memory of words or actions. Drowning sorrows does not appear to work for more than a few hours. You can rewind this 'tape' and view it with a critical eye. You can laugh at its absurdity. You can freeze the frame to remember important moments. It just seems that **you cannot wipe the tape** completely free of the original stuff. Which is fortunate, or else you'd wipe the good things too.

YOU CAN become aware of the negative loop you may be caught in and work to reverse it. In order to change, you have to become aware of a problem – and with a low self-image, you may never get that insight. You have to notice (or have someone point out to you) that you have reacted negatively to some positive suggestion. It's easy to be caught in a cycle of self-destruction.

YOU CAN seek advice and listen to constructive feedback from positive people. All too sad are the people who are never going to be around different, positive, life-affirming people who might give them a different perspective on themselves. How would you know you have been around very negative people if you never meet their positive opposites? What if negative talk and feedback is all you know? You would only think that this kind of conversation was life itself. With no comparison, there is little confusion.

Be around, observe and keep relationships with people who have a healthy self-image.

One of the very best ways to lift yourself out of the low self-image trap is to *be around, observe and keep relationships with people who have a healthy self-image*. And get as far away as you can from the people and situations that pull you down. Walk as far as you can from anyone who wants to convince, persuade or suggest to you that you're not a worthwhile human being.

"Unless and until something changes their view, unless they grasp the striking fact that they are tied with a thread, that the chain is an illusion, that they were fooled, and ultimately, that whoever so fooled them was wrong about them and that they were wrong about themselves – until all this happens, these children are not likely to show society their positive attributes as adults."

Gavin de Becker

To work on a low self-image, you have to stand in a different place and look at your life. Did you apply for dead-end jobs? If so, why? Did you apply for scholarships or trainee schemes? If so, why? Did you read the ad that said 'we're looking for a motivated and capable person' and turn the page? Did you knock on the door of an employer and ask about vacancies, knowing that you could handle the rejection if it came? You have to really think about your responses. If you're caught in a cycle of doom and gloom, then it may take a real push to get yourself out of it.

Pointing to the past and saying 'they might have been wrong about me' is not an easy thing to do. It's so hard in fact, that '. . . if the evidence of our senses runs contrary to our picture of self, then that evidence is distorted. In other words, we cannot see all that our senses report but only the things which fit the picture we have' (Carl Rogers). We may be confronted by 'proof' that we are OK, and reject it because it doesn't fit the image we have already accepted as the truth.

But Carl Rogers also had good news about what it takes to become a person. He advises becoming *open* to experience, so that we have a chance to take in the evidence of a new situation as it is, rather than distorting it to fit a pattern that we already hold – sometimes too dearly.

When 'an individual becomes more openly aware of his own feelings and attitudes', when he breaks down the 'rigidity and defensiveness' that can protect a lousy self-image and negative view of the world, 'he sees that not all trees are green, not all men are stern fathers, not all women are rejecting and not all failure experiences prove that he is no good . . .'

YOU CAN become more open and aware. Look and listen again. Hear about things from your own or another's point of view. It's hard to take off the filters and use all our senses but it can be done. Be honest with yourself. We are free to question. Indeed, 'the important thing', said Einstein, 'is not to stop questioning.' (There was a guy who knew about turning around some negative programming! He had been labelled a delinquent and probable loser from a tender age.)

YOU CAN input new messages. You can do this yourself. You don't need any equipment, instructions, helpers or software. You just speak hopefully and patiently with yourself.

So, the way to modify the self-image is to catch yourself doing OK and tell yourself about it. You also need to catch yourself being negative and flip the record over. **Feed in and repeat positive optimistic messages** (like the ones you stick on a fridge that say 'buy milk') **reminding you to love, laugh, try, risk, be open and be happy.** You have to be persistent to counter the negatives that pop up. It may sound like new-age psychobabble, and maybe it is, but the *only* way known to modify and override a destructively low self-image is through self-talk. It sounds silly, but what is sillier than letting exactly the same process work against you?

By the way, no one is going to lock you up. No one can hear your self-talk. And you don't have to PROVE the new messages against the 'facts' of the old messages! It was, and is, all opinion. And here's where the brain's design works in our favour. The subconscious mind records everything as 'fact'. So when you feed in *new messages* (including more positive messages) the subconscious stores those too. Of course, the front of the shop might question the new deliveries. Positive inputs may be unusual. The conscious mind may think, 'I haven't seen this before. I don't know if I've got a file for this.' But the co-operative subconscious will store those messages just the same.

As a child, you may have been a captive audience, without the means to walk away or the knowledge to counterbalance the negatives. But as an adult, you ARE free to walk away from a situation where you are being put down. As an adult you have the height and power to look someone in the face and say, 'Well, that's *your* opinion!'

As a child you listened in innocence. As an adult you are free to say, 'I'm changing my view. I'm confronting that "truth". The chain is an illusion'. Whether you use that freedom or not is another thing.

"You realise you must never make decisions in your life based on that negative voice in your head. And also that so many people do just that. You must always instead go with your primary thought, your hopeful thought. And that's what I try to do."

Billy Connolly

Getting help – turning things around

I hope you don't have a self-talk recording that is persistently playing 'B sides'. Does telling yourself that you're 'worthless, stupid, ugly, good for nothing, a waste of space or unlovable' feel normal?

Do your work choices reflect this inner belief? If you cannot even imagine how you could love your work or be happy in any kind of employment, then you may choose to get some help. The choice is there. Other people can help, listen and support and many will be pleased to do so.

But be careful. Be VERY wary of any group, individual or business that wants to help you in inappropriate ways. I would call charging around a forest, shooting people with paint guns, getting lost in caves or hurling yourself over army training walls, an inappropriate way to help turn around a low self-image. (If it's called 'fun' – then go for it.) Sitting in circles and hurling abuse at each other until tears drench the carpet is hardly useful! I would also call wallpapering your room with slogans saying 'I am a champion, I am invincible and nothing will stand in my way' inappropriate and potentially very damaging. I would call anyone who has a good feel of your wallet as they offer to help you, someone who is not out to help YOU.

To have a very low self-image is to be vulnerable. Your confidence in your own opinion is low. Your capacity to be overpowered by a group is very strong. There are people out there who know it and want to make money out of you. In fact, there are people out there looking for you. Their strategy is to break you down and build you up, giving you the illusion that they 'built' your self- esteem. (And some of these businesses make a lot of money staying *just* inside the law.)

But there are also professionals who are qualified and ethical in the self-esteem business and they can offer support. You must do the hard work yourself, but they can support you. They will not ask you to do, say, sell, beg for, leap over, climb, chant or sing anything that you don't want to.

It's not a hopeless task. It takes work and persistence, but it is not hopeless because **you are not hopeless**.

What does a healthy self-image look like?

Good signs of a healthy self-image are the ability to laugh at yourself, admit a mistake and go out of your way to make someone else feel good. A healthy self-image gives you the confidence to be yourself (which may mean being a bit different) and to hold an opinion without needing the approval of the group. A healthy self-image means that you don't need to bully or embarrass others into agreeing with you.

People with a healthy self-image feel OK about following their own path rather than the will of others. A healthy self-image spells death to one-upmanship and games that revolve around the control or humiliation of others.

People with a healthy self-image start out with the confidence to stretch forward with higher expectations. Challenges are welcome and there is an eagerness to learn. Mistakes are learning experiences. They relax. When people relax, knowledge flows freely. There is an opportunity for creativity and action. Any successful outcome feeds the inner belief that we're worthwhile. 'I did something good. I'm OK.'

People with a healthy self-image *can and do seek happiness* in their life and work. Furthermore, they can enjoy happiness and success when it comes and cope with the setbacks when they arise.

People with a healthy self-image *can and do seek happiness* in their life and work.

People with a healthy self-image speak to others as equals. They do not talk up to anyone – they do not talk down to anyone.

Success and the self-image

A healthy self-image gives us *inner* confidence, but amongst the sadder myths of our time are the notions of how 'confidence' and 'success' appear on the outer layers of a person.

"Being powerful is like being a lady. If you have to tell people you are – you ain't."

J Carr (US union leader)

What is true for power is also true for wealth, beauty, status and success. If you have to make sure everyone knows about it, it's a sure sign that you're not too familiar or comfortable with it.

A healthy self-image is NOT the same as extreme vanity. Accepting or loving 'self' is not the same as narcissism. A narcissist's self-talk is, 'Why isn't everyone looking at me? Don't they think I'm gorgeous? They dare to disagree with me? Who the hell do they think they are? Don't they KNOW who I am? My feelings are important. Theirs are not.'

Healthy self-talk is, 'This is me, warts and all. I'm not perfect. I'm still learning. My feelings are important and so are yours. We are equals in a conversation.'

Pushing people around is NOT true confidence. Real confidence gives us the capacity to listen. If I need to shove other people about in the attempt to make myself look more important or 'bigger', then I do not have a healthy self-image. It's quite likely I have a low self-image.

To watch a manager loudly belittling an employee in front of others is to watch an insecure bully. To watch someone behaving with a particular mix of pomposity and aggression, especially in public places like restaurants, aeroplanes or shops, is to witness insecurity. Wherever the receiver is unable to fight back, you're looking at a bully. A bully does not have real strength. A bully has been systematically put down elsewhere and looks for places to strike back and feel better about themselves. (This isn't an excuse by the way!)

Someone with a healthy self-image is more likely to feel that people have equal rights in a situation, or that their opinion (and indeed, existence) is no more or less valuable and precious than anyone else's.

Being beautiful or successful is hardly a guarantee of confidence and happiness. It becomes almost tedious to read about the addictions, therapy and self-loathing amongst the 'beautiful people'. And having it all doesn't give us a strong clue. It's also a familiar tune to hear, 'I had everything money could buy and I still wasn't happy. I didn't like myself very much.'

People with a healthy self-image may be very comfortable with what they have and what they've worked for. People with a healthy self-image possess something called 'unconditional positive regard', which means that they feel OK about themselves, whatever the situation. It doesn't mean they won't try hard – it means they won't hate themselves for a failure. They don't feel the need to boast about a 'win'.

Too much self-esteem?

A discussion about self-image invariably provokes the following kinds of questions.

'We talked about the person whose self-image is low. What about when it's out of whack with reality?'

'We work with this woman. She thinks she's brilliant and she isn't. Should we tell her?'

'We work with this guy. He thinks we're all in love with him and he's as vain as hell. In fact, he's kind of unattractive. Should we tell him?'

Then comes the question, 'How did they get to be like this?' (Well, you know the answer. If their self-image says it is so, IT IS SO!)

I once held a job that required me to interview a lot of salespeople. A young candidate (about 23) began his interview by showing an album he'd created called 'My Life – A Success Story'. The opening page showed a picture of a baby on a rug. He stared at me, quite earnestly, saying, 'As you see, the look of a champion.' (It got worse.)

After a similar interview, a rejected applicant rang to say, 'There must be a mistake. I've just opened one of these rejection letters. I think somebody's messed up badly.'

I said, 'Thank you very much for applying but we had a tremendous response . . .'

I was cut off.

He chuckled, 'I'm sorry. Let me start again. You're rejecting ME? Do you realize WHO I am?'

(I should add that both of these job candidates had been through intensive sales training courses in their organizations! I would guess they'd done the 'paintball warrior' weekends too.)

A former boss of mine would sometimes scribble on a CV 'A>AxCF'. It was code for 'aspirations exceed abilities by a considerable factor'. It usually appeared after an interview where he'd encountered arrogant and pompous *behaviour*. And we're judged on our behaviour. My boss presumed this 'arrogance' might have a detrimental effect on the person's ability to manage others or work in a team. Did he feel the need to tell them? No. Did they get the job? No.

Do you need to tell someone that their opinion of themselves is too high? What exactly would you say? How do we know for sure? Does it matter? Most of the time, you can let it go because it's just irritating rather than seriously harmful in any way. You might also let the behaviour go because it hurts their chances more than it affects yours.

Are these behaviours consistent with feeling OK? Aren't they about insecurity, which is the *inability* to accept self?

If a person's insecurity and boastfulness is causing a *real* problem somewhere, then there are ways to *demonstrate reality*. Sometimes in work situations it does matter because a person has higher aspirations than their actual performance merits and their frustration is leading to work problems.

Invariably, we are confronted with our actual performance and tangible results. (In the smarter companies it happens.)

Usually the issue is for managers to deal with, and we all hope that professional managers understand the importance of separating results from wind. The conversation, if it has to happen, has *to stick to facts and demonstrable results*. A smart manager would never talk about 'intelligence' or 'potential' with an employee. (Think it – yes. Say it aloud – no!)

A person may find out at some point that their self-image is inconsistent with reality. These can be painful but necessary experiences if we are to grow. Good mental health relies on having an objective view of reality.

But if my colleague thinks he's gorgeous and he's kind of plain, well, what does it matter? To some extent, these delusions keep us going.

Is it possible for someone to go a long way on pure confidence? The answer is, *absolutely!* Look around you.

Is it possible for truly talented people to be wasting away somewhere, for want of confidence? Answer again, *absolutely!* Look around you. *But don't let it BE you.*

It's not what you are that holds you back. It's what you think you're not. Your working life will be fuelled by your self-image.

No human being is simple and robotic. You are attached to a self-image and it impacts your life; like it or lump it. It had an immediate and significant impact on every working day you ever had. It will impact every future day.

Loving your work and feeling a sense of satisfaction is going to be a struggle if somewhere inside you a voice says, 'I'm not OK. I don't deserve to be happy. I'll never be good at anything. Who loves work? Certainly not someone LIKE ME.'

It will be a challenge, but less of a dispiriting struggle, if the voice says 'I'm OK. I can do some things well. *I can give it a try*. I can learn. I'm sure I can cope. Why not me? Others do. If a thing is possible, I'm sure I can do it.'

"The words: 'I am . . .' are potent words; be careful what you hitch them to. The thing you're claiming has a way of reaching back and claiming you."

A I Kitselman

Take care of your 'self'.

CHAPTER 5

THE PEOPLE FACTOR

how to get along with the
people you work with

"Without tolerance, our world turns into hell."

Freidrich Dürrenmatt

It's interesting how we say things like:

'It's not the job. It's the people who drive me crazy.'

'If it wasn't for the politics, I wouldn't mind the work.'

Or the converse:

'The job's not much, but the people are great.'

'The work's pretty boring, but we have a good laugh.'

It seems that people can make or break our feelings towards the work we do.

Know that if you're dreaming of a job without hassle from people or 'minus office politics', then that is a dream. That job does not exist. Where you find people, you'll find politics, communication issues, conflicts and emotions. You cannot remove people from the work equation.

It's a huge bonus to find a workplace where you genuinely enjoy the company of your co-workers. It's even better to work amongst people who inspire you. But you needn't reject the job if the atmosphere isn't ideal. (If it feels like you're in the middle of a knife-throwing contest – it might be wise to leave!)

You DON'T have to like and love the people you work with. It's not reasonable to expect everyone to get along all the time. But just because you're not required to love and like your colleagues, it doesn't mean you're excused from having good manners or from *trying* to get along.

You DO have to be able to work with people. A conflict is not a problem until it hampers the work or makes it impossible to complete the task. Never set out to be on anyone's bad side. Imagine the psychopath colleague who wants everyone to 'be afraid. Be *very* afraid.'

Even if you're a loner, you still need to aim for 'productive' relationships because you won't get other people's co-operation unless they *want* to give it to you. You cannot do it all on your own. You need the help of other people, and that means *everyone*. You won't get help if you behave badly or put people down. And people like to think there's something in it for them. (This is, curiously, how the world works.)

Again, there's no need to win the staff popularity contest, but 'pleasant' and 'well-mannered' behaviours are awfully useful.

Conflict is just a word meaning 'difference'. In the workplace, conflicts can range from two different opinions on how to solve something, harmless banter and occasional spats right through to destructive cycles of emotional abuse. I've watched people get to the point of breakdown and illness over clashes with other human beings. I reached a point myself where I could barely look at one colleague without feeling nauseated. I still believe that the 'difficulties' are *rarely* deliberate. Typically the 'abuser' is ignorant of the impact they have had or of better ways to behave.

Some people are just plain afraid. They want to fix the people problems they have at work, but don't know how.

They would like things to be better but they don't know if they have the energy or skill to make a start. They worry that their attempts will make everything worse. They worry about handling the other person's responses if they start a discussion about the problem. They don't want to be seen as the problem but may have found themselves in a pit from which they cannot seem to climb out. They often wish they were skilful communicators, but are labouring under the myth that it's a talent that a lucky few are born with. Even at the psychotic end of the problem, I believe that insecurity and ignorance are more evident than a malicious desire to wound.

The worst offenders have emerged (just like us) from education systems that spent hundreds of hours on things they would never need to apply in life and failed to devote a single minute to basic interpersonal skills or the management of stress, emotion and conflict.

Getting along with people

What if YOU are the problem?

What if you are causing the people problems you're experiencing? (You should always start here first. It might not be you, but then again . . .) None of us like to think that we're the cause of any problem, but the simple truth is that all of us could get better at the 'people stuff' – and be more successful and happier as a result.

All of us could get better at the 'people stuff' – and be more successful and happier as a result.

Getting the best from other people

So, how do you get better at getting the best from other people?

Three key things will help.

1. Understanding how people work

2. Good communication skills

3. Flawless manners

Sounds simple in theory but everyone can improve in these three things.

Understanding how people work

A little knowledge is not a dangerous thing. It might bring some understanding and tolerance. It could shed a bit of light on what remains a minefield in the workplace – trying to get along with the people you work with.

Understanding people is not an exact science, largely because people are so complex, unpredictable and individual. We are different and yet we have some common ground.

Here are a dozen fairly useful (and usually fair) things about people that might help you through sticky situations at work.

1. People are terrific.

It works in your favour to start out with that assumption. It's occasionally incorrect. Don't allow the minority to affect the way you approach the majority. Appeal to someone's better nature, and it's usually delivered up. If you approach people with courtesy and respect for their competence, a small miracle occurs. You find that most people are courteous to you in return and surprisingly helpful. Or try rudeness and contempt and see the reverse 'miracle' effect.

2. People make mistakes.

There are very few genuine saboteurs who deliberately put in a lousy effort or scupper the work of others for some destructive aim. People usually do their best and try to get things right. Good tries and human mistakes (born out of good intentions) are easy to forgive and help us learn. Repeated, mischievous or malicious 'mistakes' are a different thing.

3. People experience anger, fear, sadness and joy.

We all have feelings. Emotions will be demonstrated in vastly different ways and the things that provoke these emotions will vary. Almost everyone has a sense of humour – but, of course, it comes in all kinds of packages. Nobody leaves their emotions in a locker as they come into the building.

4. People have hopes and dreams.

Take the time to listen to people and you discover their hugely varied interests, talents, experiences and ambitions. We're motivated and inspired by different things. You will have your own goals. It's wise to respect the hopes of others and let them be.

5. People see things differently.

We may both look at the same thing, but the image that hits my brain is not the same as the image that hits yours. That often means that we will react differently. That also means that we will remember things differently. And just to make life interesting, our memories aren't perfect.

6. People do think about things and try to make good decisions.

They may arrive at a decision that is different to the one you would make. Their decisions and their lives make sense to them. They are consulting a lifetime of experience and weighing that up with their own needs and wants.

7. People want to be heroes of their own lives.

Most of your colleagues have people that they are proud of. They usually want to be heroes in the eyes of those they love. It's not a good idea to stop at a desktop photo of someone's kids and say, 'Whoa – ugly little buggers, aren't they!', or make similarly tactless, unnecessary remarks about personal lives and loved ones.

8. People like recognition and attention.

Nature abhors a vacuum. At work, people like to be noticed. They do like to know how they're doing. Like plants, we wilt and die without attention. The overwhelming majority of people like to know what's going on and how their efforts contribute to the bigger picture.

9. People like to feel connected.

We like to feel connected to someone or some group. We like to find common ground with others. We huddle and form cliques very easily.

10. People dislike being rejected, humiliated and embarrassed.

We usually enjoy learning new things and can learn very quickly if we're not made to feel like a dork in the process. Destructive criticism or ridicule burns on a person's memory and the shame can inspire us to do some pretty dreadful things. We can be fooled into thinking that ridicule and pain does not do damage because we have not (yet) felt or seen the effect of it.

11. People like some degree of control.

We like to control our own lives and the situations we are in. We might go to some lengths to avoid feeling that we've lost something, or that it has been taken away without our permission. Rapid change and instability bring fear of the unknown and a sense of being out of control. Major distress can result from feeling pushed, bullied or just believing that there are no options.

And most importantly:

12. You are no better or worse than anyone around you.

We have a natural dislike for being spoken down to. We'll never be true equals in abilities, wealth, physical strengths or gifts. But you are not better, higher or mightier than the people who work beside you. You are no lower, less worthy or significant than the people who work beside you. So when you talk to people, **do not speak up or down to anyone**. Talk as an equal, with respect and a well-mannered sense of humour.

You can always find someone who contradicts these general observations, but keeping these things in mind when you deal with people could reduce a lot of grief and aggravation in your working life.

Also know this: when someone behaves 'badly' it may be because one or several of these things have been violated in some way. Perhaps the person feels out of control. Perhaps they're not getting any recognition. Perhaps they're feeling emotional about something that you don't understand. That doesn't excuse their behaviour, but it helps if you remember there's a cause behind an action.

It's terribly easy to read through a list like that and say to yourself, 'I feel that way. I wish people would treat me accordingly.' But consider how you treat the people you work with.

Good communication skills

There is no perfect communicator. It's a skill that needs constant review. Brush up on the basics and your chance of getting along with other people improves enormously. You will always have differences of opinion, but it doesn't need to degenerate into Armageddon if you or the other party can listen and speak calmly.

Listen

Good listeners quieten their voice. This means mentally strangling yourself and holding back the overwhelming desire to speak. Good listening forces you to centre the conversation on the other person and *genuinely try to understand what they're saying*. It's a rare skill. We're often assembling the next sentence in our heads. If we think our next sentence is just too wonderful to hold in, we might even interrupt or jump in at the very first opportunity.

Good listening forces you to centre the conversation on the other person and genuinely try to understand what they're saying.

'Active listening' sometimes means making noises or gestures to indicate that you're interested. It can mean being comfortable with a pause and not feeling that you have to fill the airtime.

People love being heard. It's the nicest kind of recognition. (And conversely, we get cheesed off when we feel ignored or interrupted.) Good listening makes people feel freer to be open and honest. They tend to think the listener is a decent and thoughtful person. They're more likely to feel like co-operating and listening to you in return.

A tip for the ambitious – people are more likely to assume you're intelligent if you're a good listener. Smart people speak less and say more. Or to borrow another old saying, 'It's better to remain silent and be thought a fool, than to speak out and remove all doubt.'

Question

Questions that are relevant or comments that sum up the other person's view from time to time also show that you're focused on the other person. Clever communicators also know that the person who is asking the questions is the real controller of the conversation. Knowing how to switch between the different types of questions is one of their skills.

Open questions require a person to talk a bit. (What do you think would be the best way to deal with this?) They are great for getting someone to 'open up'.

Closed questions require one word answers. (Did you speak to the customer or didn't you?) Closed questions are useful when you're trying to shut someone up or perhaps focus someone who is going off on a tangent.

Probing questions follow up something the other person has said. A probing question asks for more information. (Why did you feel that way?) Probing questions are great because they continue to open up conversation and *show interest*. (They can also backfire if the other person feels that they're getting the third degree!)

Clever communicators avoid asking leading questions, which are manipulative. They corner the other person into giving the answer you have already hinted they should give. Work isn't a TV courtroom drama. We're not interested in trapping or badgering people in our conversations.

Multiple questions overload the person, so they don't know where to start. (Tell me about yourself, why you came to work here, who you worked for in the last five years and what you liked about those employers?) Multiple questions leave us scratching our heads and asking, 'Sorry? What was the question?'

Rhetorical questions don't require an answer. So why ask them? They have some humour and drama value, but are otherwise fairly deadening. (Why do I keep coming up with rhetorical questions?)

Be aware of your body and voice

The words we choose make up a tiny percentage of the whole message being delivered. In fact, the meaning of the actual words can be completely scrubbed out by conflicting body language (eye contact, posture, gestures and subtle movements) and the meanings that are carried by our voices. A message can be completely altered just by changing the speed, pitch, volume, modulation and, importantly, tone of the voice.

These two other factors (body language and tone) are the more powerful parts of any message and their potentially damaging effect can be why some people wonder why they're so frequently misunderstood. 'Actions speak louder than words.' If what I **see** and **feel** conflicts with what you're **telling** me in words, I'll trust the 'seeing and feeling' bit.

For example, a manager protests, 'Look, I say "good morning" to them every day and I always tell people they can come to me with their problems!'

However, his team says, 'Yes, but he watches his computer screen while he speaks and grunts his "good mornings". He says his door is always open, but he looks bored and irritated whenever you speak to him.'

It was the **way** you said it!

Why did you say it like **that**?

What are you **really** trying to tell me?

What do you think they **really** meant?

This doesn't mean that words are insignificant, but if you want to be very clear about something, make sure that your look and sound match the message.

Take responsibility

Good communicators know that it's up to them to make sure a message is clearly understood. They talk WITH people, not AT people. They ask for ideas and contributions. They welcome questions. They can admit they've made a mistake or that there's room for improvement. They would apologize for any confusion, even if they felt they'd been clear.

Good communicators don't sit there guessing why someone is quiet. They take the initiative and start a conversation. If they don't know someone, they introduce themselves.

They will get to someone else's level by finding out what they like to talk about and how *they* feel about things. Great communicators get *other* people talking – a point you may feel confused about if you watch some of the interviewing that sometimes takes place on TV.

Keep conflict at a constructive level

You will help any situation by staying calm, talking to the other person as an equal and being *flexible*.

I fear that the word *assertive* has been misused and abused. Assertiveness training in the 1980s sometimes had people coming back to work thinking that shouting at others, rudely demanding attention or giving someone an 'honest' earful of hurtful criticism was being assertive.

Somewhere along the line, wrong turns were made in corridors and too many people attended AGGRESSION 101. Shouting, working with a 'bunker mentality', sulking, being aloof and abusive outbursts are not signs of assertiveness.

Being assertive means talking ACROSS to people. NOT UP to them as if you're afraid and powerless and NOT DOWN to them, throwing your weight around or implying that you know best. Assertiveness is about stating what you need or want, listening to what the other person needs and wants and trying to come up with some solution that suits you both.

It also means being fairly honest. Not 'Wow, that's a big blackhead on your nose!', kind of honest, but straight and tactful about things that are relevant to the situation.

We shouldn't be concerned about changing our style of communication. In fact, we'd be very boring and terribly rigid if we didn't. Obviously, we communicate and behave differently at a funeral than at a party. We would not speak to a colleague in the same way that we would cheer for a team or comfort a child.

Some styles are useful at work, and some will hinder your chances. **It's not OK to be aggressive, angry and pushy. It's not OK to whine or be disruptive, sulky or bitchy.**

It is OK to laugh, have fun and create, and to be energetic, enthusiastic and open with people. Work would be dismal if we didn't laugh. But be careful! Don't overdo it or you'll come across as the office clown. People will adore you but they may also worry about your ability to finish tasks, take things seriously or deal with more salient matters. And 'fun' is not had at the expense of other people. Ridiculing or embarrassing people isn't 'fun'.

It's OK to be supportive and to coach, listen to and guide other people. What if nobody showed any concern or knew how to listen? What if we could not react appropriately to someone experiencing a real problem? But again, be careful! Don't overdo it! Avoid talking down to people in a 'nice but oh so sickly way'. If you work as a nurse or teacher of small children it is entirely appropriate to be kindly, sweet and caring, but in a workplace with other adults *it can irritate.* You might 'take care' of people in some situations but you have to avoid sounding as if you're their guardian angel, sent to put plasters on knees. People don't like being spoken down to. It gets their backs up quickly if it's done in an aggressive way, but they also get annoyed if it's done in a patronising way.

It's OK to be calm, professional, well-mannered, focused on the situation and even-tempered. If in doubt or facing a very difficult person, then stay calm and keep your voice as steady as you can. This 'adult' style will usually lead you out of the mire. Asking questions and working towards a solution will keep you from getting distracted by temper. This is not the time to have fun. It is not the time to be supportive and guiding. It is the time to be level-headed and professional. (Blow off steam later, when the person is not around!) Staying calm forces the other person to play your game and that sounds terribly self-controlled, but make it a habit. Highly professional people seem to do this naturally.

Great communicators can listen effectively, use questions as tools, pay attention to their body language and voice and take responsibility. Being assertive, calm, flexible and sensitive will always help. But it starts with the attitude that this is a skill set which can be learned and must be practised.

If you can apply your skill, live with the fact that people are unpredictable and understand that you'll never have an absolutely perfect day – then you may turn out to be a terrific communicator.

And then people may say of you: 'she could put anyone at their ease' or 'he could talk with anyone about anything' or 'they made you feel the centre of attention'. They may even say that 'you always manage to say and do the right thing'. (And if they say this, it probably means that you're also very well mannered.)

A quick guide to flawless manners

Etiquette books are great for advice on folding napkins, sending wedding invitations and placing glasses on tables.

But they don't help us very much with problems that arise in the modern workplace.

With means (and speeds) of communicating (ie, mobile phones and e-mails), open-plan offices and the relaxing of so many formalities these days, it may be hard to know whether you're being brief and efficient or abrupt and offensive. Very few people would enjoy being labelled an 'ignorant pig', but an astonishing number of people can carry this reputation without realizing it and would be mortified if they knew.

When you're working hard and fast, it's not possible to consider every word and the possible implications, but there are some really useful rules of thumb that'll make sure people respond very positively to you.

- However busy you are, don't forget to say *please* and *thank you*. They go a long way.

- When working with others, recognize a favour or contribution when you see it and give credit where it's due. Ask politely for something to be done. Apologizing and admitting a problem (or mistake) goes down a treat.

- Stick around to help with the grubby end of a task and don't leave that to others. Know how to offer assistance when you see it might be needed, without being patronizing.

- Respect people's space and say 'excuse me' if you need to interrupt. Don't speak loudly or make a lot of noise when people are trying to work. Don't use a mobile phone in any place where people are forced to listen to the conversation.

- Don't pull rank. Treat *everyone* with respect and earn respect in return.

- Try not to swear all the time but save it for appropriate occasions.

- Be generous with your knowledge, attention span and sincere, relevant praise.

- Start a conversation with someone you don't know and focus the talk on that person's interests. Ask questions and look interested.

- Say 'hello' or 'good night, everyone' or acknowledge the people around you in some way.

- Arrive on time for meetings or apologize if you're late.

- Build on ideas and listen to others, rather than indulging in games or displays of one-upmanship.

- Acknowledge everyone and introduce yourself. Close conversations with the appropriate handshake or 'thank you'.

- Observe a simple rule about e-mails, memos and texts that is worth knowing: If you wouldn't say it – don't type it.

If you want to earn the tag of 'ignorant pig' it's really not that difficult. You could try some simple and quick techniques like these.

- Do not consider the workload of others – because it's not relevant to your world.

- React indignantly or make fun of someone who makes a polite request of you, for example, 'Do you mind keeping the noise down?'

- Read, type, hold a phone to your ear or look elsewhere when someone is trying to talk to you.

- Interrupt or talk over whoever is speaking and do not take account of what's been said.

- Hold another conversation on a mobile whilst in a meeting or even take work into a meeting because you're 'too busy for the boring bits'.

- Ring in for messages or carry on 'texting' in meetings.

- Conduct 'side' conversations in meetings.

- Instantly overreact to e-mails that are sent to you and quickly shoot something even more offensive back – but copy in lots of people just to get them 'on side'.

- Use e-mail for everything and copy people in on messages to 'cover your arse' all the time.

- Reach for a ringing phone or mobile in mid conversation.

- Let other people's phones ring unanswered.

- Answer a phone with 'Yeah?', 'What?' or 'Speak!'

- Fail to close the conversation politely.

- Continue to use a keyboard while on the phone.

Ralph Waldo Emerson wrote that 'Good manners are made up of petty sacrifices.' The well mannered are prepared to take the path of least offence, to make the first move and to let go of that voice in the head which screams, 'Overpower, shout louder, do what the infant in you wants to do.'

There are so many things we do which could offend other people because we all have different standards of behaviour. As a general rule, if you're not sure – ask. If someone makes a request – respond to it politely. If you've caused offence – or believe you have – apologize.

CHAPTER 6

WHAT TO DO WHEN IT ALL GETS TRICKY

handling conflict and anger

"Men are disturbed not by things that happen but by their opinion of the things that happen."

Epictetus

How to speak up for yourself

Conflict is so normal that workplaces without it are probably in trouble. If everyone is in constant agreement, it only means that people are not speaking up. We know that people think differently. If they don't air their opinions, it might be that they're afraid to or don't care to. Either way, you have the symptoms of rot in the workplace.

Sadly, some managers think they're fabulously efficient if people agree with them all the time, without having the faintest idea that they're on a slippery slope. If you and your colleagues *always* agree, then some of you needn't be there.

Conflict need not be hostile, aggressive or unpleasant. There's no reason why it shouldn't be a very normal process with a calm conversation. So much depends on our personal feelings about conflict and how a situation is managed or approached.

In a *constructive conflict* everyone is aiming for the best possible outcome. People try to build on each other's ideas, agreeing where possible and disagreeing in a calm and rational manner. Generally, voices are normal (or calmer) and contributions are in the way of facts, doubts, concerns and questions. Humour and enthusiasm are welcome. Smug arrogance and aggression are not. Comments are more thought-provoking than provocative.

Trying to get an outcome that suits all parties (and it's never perfect) is not just a nice theory about making everyone feel warm and cuddly. It is common sense. It makes good commercial sense. If someone walks away from a conflict feeling that they have lost, then there WILL be consequences. Generally, people don't like that feeling and will go to some lengths to avoid it or make up for it.

Speaking up when you're concerned or angry is a valuable thing to do. Speaking up for progress or to challenge complacency keeps a business alive. It is also a way of protecting and preserving. It's a way of defending ethics and values, and preventing careless change. There are times to push hard for the things you believe in.

Speaking up when you're concerned or angry is a valuable thing to do.

HOW you do this is important, and *destructive conflict* is the thing to avoid. In destructive conflicts, people try to line up on the 'good' and 'bad' sides. ('They are the bad guys and we are the good guys.') There is little concern about long-term effects or the other side's needs and wants. Blaming and one-upmanship are present.

Destructive conflicts get personal. Destructive conflicts can descend into a misery game called 'who shouts loudest wins'. In destructive conflicts, people are rarely listening. They are marshalling their responses ready to jump in (sometimes just interrupting or speaking over others) at the first opportunity. In a destructive conflict, the only real listening and thinking may be carried out with the aim of destroying the 'other' side, denying facts, getting counter-arguments ready and only putting forward information which might help to 'win'. That's dangerous because all kinds of information may be necessary to find the best solution.

In a destructive conflict, everyone thinks there will be a winner and a loser, and they don't want to be the loser. Nobody wins it in the long run though, because bitterness and regret prevail. All the while, everyone's eyes are off the main target, which is improvement.

Some will be sulking. Some will be angry over the inability to focus on what is important, believing that the team is arguing over petty detail. Some will be biding their time or playing games. Some will be red-faced and frustrated and a few will be having the times of their lives.

But the worst thing about destructive conflicts is the WASTE OF TIME, MONEY AND ENERGY. Destructive conflicts can sacrifice progress because people are not moving forward. Destructive conflicts don't just cause people to dislike their work, they can cause people to leave it for the wrong reasons, sabotage other people's efforts, sabotage their OWN efforts (to block someone else) or become sick from all the bad feeling which hangs in the air.

Destructive conflicts make it impossible to love your work.

How to avoid destructive conflicts at work

1. Don't engage in right v wrong too quickly (and don't get so worried about being wrong)

'Well hang on – if I see it this way – and he sees it that way – then ONE of us must be wrong!' We can be so easily threatened by a difference. We may be too well schooled in the idea that if we are right (and we like to be right) then someone else with a different idea must be wrong.

We assume there must be a right decision. (Sometimes there's only a best way for the moment.) We assume that every problem has an answer. (It may not). We assume that there's ONE answer. (There might be several.)

We assume that there are two sides to everything. (That's not always the case and trying to find the other side could be a waste of time. Time could be better spent building on an idea.)

We can go to absurd lengths to protect ourselves from being wrong – as if it's the worst thing in the world. It really isn't so frightening to say, 'You're right. I never thought of it that way.' It's completely irrational to believe you have to be right and perfect all the time. It's not possible.

Survival depends on flexibility and adaptation. A wise person admits a mistake and learns from it.

2. Remember that work is not war

Business is not the same as war no matter how many macho, melodramatic and warlike portrayals of business get thrown our way. We have brought too many war metaphors (even calling boardrooms 'war rooms') into our working-day language. In doing this, unnecessary and confusing pressure is put on people to behave ridiculously and (usually) counter-productively. 'He lacks the killer instinct.' 'I need to talk to the troops.' 'The front line.' 'Shot down in a meeting.' 'Going in to do battle.' 'Going in guns blazing.' 'Going off half-cocked.'

There are team training programmes that emulate war games – leaping over walls, shooting pellet guns, chanting war cries and wearing khaki. It is nonsense to believe that this improves the chances for constructive conflict at work.

In war there is a clear objective. Discipline, obedience and directed aggression are vital. Disabling the enemy is paramount. Certainly there are some lessons that can be applied WITH CARE from military history. (Military blunders and the dangers of 'groupthink' are an even richer source of learning!)

Business is about financially *surviving* the long term. In business, we strive to create relationships or reputations that make people WANT to deal with us and work for us. Business is about adapting, developing, being free to trade and encouraging people to think differently. Customers do not stay with a business because they've been defeated and ordered to buy from them. Employees do not give a business their best because they fear a court martial or enemy fire.

In war, the opposition is dehumanized. It makes people easier to kill if you can forget they are human beings. (Try operating like that in a workplace or business market for any length of time.)

In the workplace we falter and stumble if we dehumanize those we deal with. Usually we do this by lumping them together in some non-human description. 'Oh that's typical of Accounts!' 'That would have to be Sales again!'

In a conflict rut, we might develop nicknames for groups that we dislike. Again, time and effort is being wasted. The organization has a sickness. It then requires a small breakthrough for people to come together. It should never be a shock to discover that our colleagues are human beings and not our enemies.

Working (for most people) is more akin to building than it is to soldiering. Businesses need more creators and fewer destroyers. Businesses need more thinkers and fewer windbags. We all need less competitive b*** s*** within the workplace. It doesn't seem to be making anyone happier or more productive and it's certainly irritating the quiet achievers.

There never was a 'good' war but there are plenty of good ways to work and conduct business.

3. Aggression isn't necessary (or sexy) to demonstrate effectiveness

In the movie *Broadcast News*, Holly Hunter plays a news producer who, while under pressure and being observed by a senior manager, screams down her phone at the studio's car park attendant. Wanting a guest to be let into the studio grounds, she stands up and becomes hysterical. 'Do it! Do it! Do it or I'll fry your fat ass!'

The executive turns to another and says, 'My God! I had no *idea* she was this good!' Of course – it's only a movie. In the real world, surely nobody thinks that a tantrum indicates a high performer? How would noise, rudeness, dramatics and extreme behaviour actually help achieve a result?

It MIGHT be that some good performers behave this way, but every time they do, they extract goodwill from the people they attack. It costs them. They need an awful lot of goodwill to do this over a long period and hold on to other people's co-operation. A noise is not a result. The whistle does NOT drive the train.

4. We leap into anger because we don't know better

"We are all captives of the pictures in our head – our belief that the world we have experienced is the world that really exists."

Walter Lippman

During one house move, while standing in a kitchen full of packing cartons and paper, a new cooker was delivered without the necessary connections to make it work. The removal company foreman caught me in a mild state of panic and I told him my dilemma.

He started shouting, 'There's only ONE way to deal with people like that. You get on that phone and tell those ****'s to get back here or I'll ****ing break their ****ing arms.' (You get the picture!)

Without even knowing the situation or the probability I *had* been told the stove would not be ready (and I'd forgotten it), he assured me this would be the only way to get a result. And he's not alone. There are a lot of people who think that attack is the FIRST and only practical option. Shout! Scream! Don't let them get a word in! Offence is the best defence. Get in first and tell them what's what!

It's what they've been taught. It doesn't work, but the attacker usually puts that down to 'difficult people' (you just can't tell some people) rather than faulty learning. It's not easy to question your lifetime's 'journey', even if it was undertaken with a cracked compass.

Try talking to this man about his 'influencing strategy' and I predict that his first comment would be, 'This constructive conflict stuff is all very well in theory, but in the real world . . .'

In the real world, people do not co-operate with you unless they want to. They rarely want to co-operate if they dislike you. That is not to say that anyone is ever free from conflict situations. The trick is to get conflicts to the CONSTRUC-TIVE level as quickly and as often as you possibly can.

To do that, you'll need to be a good communicator, understand people and possess good manners. But you also need to understand the value of constructive conflict and the need for *building solutions* rather than fighting corners. Appreciate the value in getting people's buy-in, or commitment, and if time does not permit that, at least understand other people's need to question what's going on and air their concerns. This will keep most conflicts on a steady and workable level.

What about impossible situations?

What if you try all of the above and repeatedly fail?

There are times when the most tolerant and effective human beings face problems with other people's behaviour.

And that leads to a whole new area.

What to do if someone at work is getting you down

You have options. Whoever it is (and it could be the chairman of the board) and whatever your role is at work, you're not powerless. But you need to be organized. Impulsive outbursts are very tempting but they usually make things worse. Before you act, think.

First, some soul-searching questions.

→ Is it your reactions that are causing the problem?
Could you be overreacting? Is there some particular trigger here that is very personal to you because of your life experiences? That's not to say you're wrong to feel the way you do, but sometimes it helps to ask ourselves why we're so bothered.

→ Is it a significant problem affecting your work or is it just irritating?
Can you live with this? Is it so bad that it's making you miserable? We don't have to like and love the people we work with but we *do need* to have productive working relationships. Can you, at least, work together?

→ How exactly does this problem impact your work?
Can the impact be demonstrated? Say it out loud to yourself or to someone you trust – 'The person's behaviour is an issue because . . .' (A problem well defined may not be half solved, but it's an excellent start.)

→ What have you done about it?
Have you genuinely tried to talk to this person about the

situation? You cannot delegate the responsibility of fixing breakdowns to other people unless it's a very serious behaviour problem and you have no means of tackling it on your own.

→ Is it possible that you're contributing to this situation in some way?

Because in ongoing relationships, the way people behave towards you is usually dictated by the way you behave towards them. Is it possible that you are doing exactly the same things that you find so disagreeable? Do other people experience this behaviour from you?

→ What are you prepared to do about it? Do you care enough?

At what point would you give up trying to solve it? Are you prepared to leave? Are you prepared for a possible stormy response and fall-out?

OK. Now you're a little more organized than just saying, 'They get up my nose!'

(Arguments over personal beliefs are *not* for the workplace. A colleague's sexual preferences, choices in religion, politics, football team and choice of toothpaste are PERSONAL. We don't need to know and we certainly shouldn't be engaged in workplace conflicts about this stuff.)

You have a choice – do something or don't.

Option 1 – doing something

You could confront the 'difficult person' head on, or try the slower road of influence. Either way – you need to think first and plan.

Talking to the person who you're in conflict with can be the fastest, most direct path to a change for the better. But it has the potential for disaster, which is why we may shrink from trying it.

Increase the chances of a successful resolution

Pick your time and place

Ask to see the person in private. These conversations should never take place in front of others.

Don't attack

Don't get into personal criticism or insult opinions, or even use snide, dismissive comments such as 'you would say something like that'. In short, don't antagonise! If you're trying to be mean, then attacking works, because it IS mean. If you're trying to fix a situation or persuade someone to your way of thinking, attacking doesn't work. If you need to have long-term contact with this person, then meanness guarantees that what you've said will come back to haunt you in some way.

An insult only demonstrates your lack of self-control at that moment. In any case, how will a direct insult change things? We're not going to agree with a cutting remark and we rarely agree with people who hurt us. Being negative only tells people what NOT to do. Don't attack. It doesn't work.

Say what you feel

You can confront a situation without being confrontational. Say what you feel but say it calmly. Rehearse it.

Imagine what the responses might be. There might be agreement or all hell might break loose. Listen to what the other person has to say, without interrupting.

Maybe they appear unhelpful because you always ask them for help when they are snowed under. Maybe they just didn't realize. Maybe they thought it was OK because no one ever said anything before.

I once told a colleague that I found his daily assessments and comments on my clothes patronizing and I was sure it wasn't his intention to be rude. I also said that I wouldn't comment on what he was wearing. (It was tempting. He liked purple bell-bottoms.) He was most apologetic. A previous female colleague used to sulk if he did NOT comment on her wardrobe for the day. Poor guy! How confusing!

Present your case as your perception

Say 'I FEEL' rather than 'YOU ARE'. Don't speak as if it's fact.

Never throw in 'everyone else thinks so too'. (Even if everyone else does, that comment is REALLY mean and unhelpful.) It is far less threatening (and therefore easier to make change possible) if the other person does not feel cornered.

What is the change you want to see?

What is the other person DOING or SAYING that is causing you a problem? Don't talk about their attitude. You can't see an attitude. Don't talk about personality. You can't see that either. Talk about *observable behaviour*. Then you need to be clear about *what you'd like to see instead*. Don't assume that stating a problem will lead them to the obvious change. If it were obvious, they'd be doing it. And when people are trying to change (as this person might be) it helps to have a target in mind.

What is the change you don't want to see?

You don't want people to throw away their good habits or feel that you're criticizing everything about them. It's useful to say something that you appreciate about their behaviour. (Let's hope you can find something.)

'Would it be possible?' 'Do you think . . .?'

Phrasing what you want as a question is helpful. It has an air of choice and freedom about it. You're not telling the person what to do – you're offering a suggestion and that's a very different thing. A question (that allows a person to explain) delivered in a calm and steady voice, is far more effective than a closed insult. A question allows the person to think and POSSIBLY meet you halfway with an answer or a question of their own.

"The most immutable barrier in nature is between one man's thoughts and another's."

William James

You have to make another person realize that their behaviour has caused you a problem. You cannot do someone else's thinking for them. They're MORE likely to listen to you if they think you have listened to them. They're MORE likely to consider your opinion if they believe that you've considered theirs.

Leave things for a while

And thank the person for listening. Leave it for a while. Give them some time to think.

Try the most assertive and polite approach first. Try it again if you didn't succeed first time. Then, if you feel you have to raise your voice a bit, you can honestly say, 'I have been trying to tell you.' You rarely need to raise your voice if you use this approach with sincerity.

If all hell breaks loose, at least you tried. Don't add fuel to the fire. Just extract yourself from the situation with dignity. You can walk away feeling brave because you were. Better to have tried. You will probably have learned something along the way. Give it time before you call the experience a failure. The other person may be thinking over what you said and it may take time, but you could see the beginnings of a change.

Is it easier to put up with a bad situation and get worn down by it, than to do something about it? I would always cheer for the person who acts. This is the brave option.

The biggest surprise is that you can be prepared for the *worst* possible reaction and find the person apologizing – they hadn't realized how their behaviour was affecting you. People rarely mean to cause distress in the workplace.

Use the slower road of influence

We can't instantly change someone's behaviour, but it is possible to influence a person over time. We can shape someone's behaviour, without telling them what we're up to.

First – we lead by example. Secondly, we use attention or 'rewards' when we catch them doing right. For example, if the problem is rudeness, and I want the other person to use 'please' and 'thank you', then it is critical that I always use good manners when I'm dealing with them. We learn by aping. Modelling alone can produce the desired effect.

When they DO say 'please' or 'thank you', catch that moment and smile, say something like 'you're very welcome' and generally make it more likely that they will continue with this new 'skill'. Sounds simple and it is. It's the way most of us are trained and schooled. It's called 'learning' and it's how so much of our behaviour becomes a habit. We do and say as we have seen and as we have been rewarded.

Certainly there will be no change at all if I behave exactly the way that this 'difficult' person does. 'Behaviour breeds behaviour.' There will also be no change if I make fun of their attempts to change, use sarcasm or behave negatively toward them. (Then they're not going to care what I think and they're not going to seek my attention.)

Some people will advise you to 'give as good as you get'. I would question that. I would say 'give as you would LIKE

Remember that people seek connection, love recognition and attention, dislike ridicule and embarrassment and care what others think about them.

to get'. Many people advise you to 'fight fire with fire'. Last time I checked, that didn't put a fire out.

Remember that people seek connection, love recognition and attention, dislike ridicule and embarrassment and care what others think about them. Put all that together and you have a clue as to what works (and what doesn't) in the change 'toolbox'.

Option 2 – leave it (try to cope or rise above it)

In our personal lives, when we see no hope, we can remove ourselves from relationships and situations or cut contact with people who have hurt us. We can also leave our work and lose all contact, but we may not wish to end what is otherwise a good situation. You may decide you don't wish to confront. Maybe it's a short-term thing. Perhaps you're planning to leave and you think it's not worth it. Perhaps you know the other person is planning to leave and you feel you can wait. Perhaps you tried and nothing seemed to work. There are situations where you try everything decent and rational and it gets you nowhere.

Coping strategies

You'll need some kind of mantra, or coping strategy, that helps you to stifle the urge to explode or cheerfully strangle the person who provokes you.

Here are some ideas for 'rising above it'.

1. 'That which does not destroy me makes me stronger.'
   Kate used to say this to herself when she worked for a 'nightmare' boss. He'd put his face about six inches from hers, scream abuse (often in front of other staff members or customers) and, ten minutes later, call her into his office crying, 'Why don't the other staff like me? How come they never ask me out with them?' He had her woken (while off duty) in the middle of the night to lift some heavy boxes. When she asked why he couldn't handle it, as he was on duty, he shouted, 'I've just turned 40! Don't I have enough to deal with?' He had a sign behind his desk saying 'WHO OWNS THE PROBLEM?' Should any staff member see him with a concern, he'd simply point to the sign and then point to the door. Kate eventually resigned, but says this 'mantra' pulled her through the worst bits.

2. A little empathy might help.
   How do *you* look from this person's point of view? How is your life compared to theirs? It's not an excuse for their behaviour, but is it possible to calm down and think about how the world might look from their point of view?

   I had a colleague who drove me to distraction with his unhelpful, obstructive, surly behaviour. One day, I was chewing my knuckle about him to another colleague who said, 'Did you know he and his wife can't have kids? Did you know they've spent years paying off his father's debts? Did you know that his home life revolves around looking after a sick mother-in-law?' Again, it wasn't an excuse for his behaviour, which bordered on the 'disciplinary' at times, but I thought about my own life and suddenly felt extremely fortunate. I never felt quite as annoyed about him from then on.

3. Give up on *oughts* and *shoulds*.
Relax your expectations of the world a little. Yes, people OUGHT to behave in certain ways and everyone SHOULD observe standards of decency, but they don't. It's a shame, but it happens. Festering and fuming isn't going to change it. If you really feel strongly about a breach of standards at work, say something constructive and work towards change. If you don't want to do that, give up on *oughts* and *shoulds* and get on with your own life.

4. 'Never fight with pigs. they love it and you only end up getting covered in s***.'
There are people that you should avoid fighting with because it's what they're trying to provoke. There are fights that are not worth having. How many things are worth really fighting for in your working life? Decide what is important. When you know what really matters, defend it and stand your ground. Let the rest go.

5. Get some perspective. This is not a tragedy.
Say this to yourself. 'I don't get on with everyone. This is not a tragedy.' There is a world outside your workplace. Focus on something else. There are people in real pain with serious issues to contend with. And there are people out there who you DO get on with.

6. Switch focus or laugh.

   You may have to wait for the next work break to try this, but try to focus on 'feel good' things, like photos that make you happy. Do you have some music that always makes you feel good? Is there something you can read that makes you laugh? Ask yourself, 'What would my hero do?' A picture of your comedy hero's probable reaction might help you think of something funny to defuse your feelings of anger. Do you have a friend who makes you laugh? Can you call them?

7. What's up?

   If someone behaves bizarrely towards you, tell yourself that something bad must have happened and that you're the nearest person they feel able to take it out on. This is a good strategy for behaviour that is out of character or a 'one-off' outburst. Try forgiving the unusual and isolated stuff without needing to know the circumstances. If you can say to yourself, 'it's very unlikely they're trying to get at me personally' it gives you the grace to sidestep them and calm down. It also gives you the opportunity to ask, 'Is everything OK? Can I help? You don't seem your usual self.'

8. What are you afraid of?

   People can behave at their worst when they are afraid of losing something or when they feel cornered in some way. Animals are at their most dangerous when they are cornered. Animals also attack to protect their young. And so it is with human beings. We behave badly when we feel cornered or believe that something sacred (to us) is under threat. Speak calmly. Use a friendly welcoming tone in your conversation that pulls people towards you rather than pushing them into a corner. How would you walk towards a barking dog? If you think that answer through, then you know exactly what to do when confronted by a human being acting aggressively. (Barking, by the way. Not foaming at the mouth with rabies!)

9. A little sympathy rather than empathy.

"Teach me to feel another's woe,
To hide the fault I see;
That mercy I to others show
That mercy show to me."

Alexander Pope

So much 'bad' behaviour stems from jealousy and feelings of inadequacy. It's a sad person who demands that others agree with them. It's a sad person who doesn't know how to make others feel good or cannot see the value in making the workplace a fun place to be. You could switch your feelings of anger to pity.

10. Ignore the behaviour.
Behaviour can go away when it is ignored. (Sadly, that applies to 'good' behaviour as well.) The reason for this is that people seek attention. When they don't get it, they usually try something else. If you know someone is trying to get a reaction by pushing your buttons, then don't give it. Avoid or minimize contact with the very disagreeable behaviour where possible. A simple shrug and a 'so what' can confuse someone who is looking for a bigger pay-off. Bullies can give up if the pay-off doesn't come.

Ignoring doesn't always work and sometimes you have to make a stronger stand but try it in the first few instances.

"Value in action that is actionless, few indeed can understand . . . That the yielding conquers the resistant and the soft conquers the hard is a fact known by all men, but utilized by none."

Lao Tsu

11. I will decide my reactions – thank you.

    Choose how you are going to react. Just as we might fail to influence someone's thinking in one direction, so they cannot force ours. People that we come to dislike intensely have begun to have as much power over us as people we really care about. And should they influence our actions, then they have proved that power. WHY would I want to let someone I dislike have some control over my thoughts and actions? Hatred and anger require energy. To spend energy on someone is a compliment. The opposite of love is indifference.

12. A quick seethe and then move on.

    On very bad days, you could allow yourself some venting time. Writing down exactly how you feel and what you would like to say is very therapeutic – *but shred it!*

    Some people place a caricature on a dartboard, some use a picture taped to a punch bag and others sculpt little voodoo dolls out of Blu-tack. I wouldn't call any of these methods 'rising above it' – but it works for some.

When it is on the page and off your chest, say, 'OK. That's all the time I'm giving you! You've taken up enough energy', because as Ralph Waldo Emerson said, *'For every minute you are angry, you lose 60 seconds of happiness.'* What do you want to do with your life? Spend it being angry? It's your choice.

13. A quick scream at someone you can trust.

    In a bad situation some years ago, I used to call a friend who worked nearby. All I had to say was 'I *need* to do lunch' and she knew exactly what I meant. It can help to just talk it over with someone you know very well – someone who is in a calmer frame of mind and doesn't mind listening to you rant and rave from time to time. (And make sure you offer the same support to them!)

14. One day I'll look back on this and laugh.

    Reduce the significance of this moment and this person's behaviour.

    One day I'll have forgotten this moment.
    This person is 1 in 6 billion.
    This moment is a small part of one day in my life.
    This feeling will pass.
    It's not the person, it's their behaviour.

    Or try this:

    'It's all good dialogue in the screenplay of my life!'

15. Community service award.

This method requires you to keep a bag of treats in a drawer. The next time you face this difficult situation you say to yourself, 'Somewhere, a village was missing an idiot but I think I've found them. I deserve a reward.'

I used this 'mantra' with a manager who was a loud, repugnant bully. It worked for a while but I noticed I kept buying more and more chocolates for my reward drawer and the village never did show up to collect.

16. Turn it into a learning experience.

Learning to handle conflict is an important life skill. Put on an observer's hat and imagine you are studying human behaviour at its worst. As a colleague once noted, on witnessing some atrocious behaviour, 'Now I understand why some creatures eat their young.'

17. What a wonderful world.

You could try to rise above things by taking the most optimistic and humane view you possibly can. 'I will never see things the way others see them but isn't the world more interesting because we are so different? Aren't we lucky to have such diversity?' (You might find this one a bit too nauseating to cope with, I realise.)

18. Oh, I *am* sorry!

A friend, who'd worked as a stewardess for a long time, and I were discussing work. She said, 'I couldn't do what you do and face angry people all the time.' I was amazed. 'I couldn't cope with *your* work,' I said. 'I could *not* handle an aircraft full of people getting grumpy, petty or rude about things I couldn't possibly fix.'

'Oh, that's easy!' she said. 'You get used to that straightaway. Whining goes over your head. You just smile and say 'Oh I *am* sorry, sir. Can I get something else for you?' Or you thank them for bringing that to your attention. It's a habit you get into. You don't feel that saying "sorry" costs you anything. They're not being personal.'

I must add that my friend has perfect manners and is the last person you would call insincere. She simply knew how to rise above constant baiting.

19. Sing! (I'm serious)

❝Most of the men sang or whistled as they dug or hoed. There was a good deal of outdoor singing in those days. Workmen sang at their jobs; men with horses and carts sang on the road; the baker, the miller's man, and the fish-hawker sang as they went from door to door; even the doctor and parson on their rounds hummed a tune between their teeth. People were poorer and had not the comforts, amusements or knowledge we have today; but they were happier. Which seems to suggest that happiness depends more on the state of mind – and body, perhaps – than upon circumstances and events.❞

Flora Thompson – 'Lark Rise to Candleford'

My favourites are Nat King Cole's 'Pretend' and Julie London's 'Fly Me to the Moon.' On very, very bad days, I sing Carly Simon's 'I Haven't Got Time for the Pain'. A friend swears by 'Never Mind the Bollocks' by the Sex Pistols.

I have described some tips for rising above a situation, but I'm sure there are more. If you find you can recover your balance quickly and forget about it, then your strategy is working. But if you're taking the problem home and it's keeping you awake or making you ill, then it's **not working**. It may be time to do something more direct.

Don't let your work or health suffer. Sports, fun, relaxation and taking care of yourself are going to be important if you decide to go for this option and the situation is ongoing.

Sabotage

From time to time I have heard someone brag about their clever idea for 'getting their own back'. This usually involves some kind of sabotage or childish revenge game. The person justifies it, saying it helps them 'rise above it' but if it's taking up time and energy, then it's not turning a blind eye. It's beneath you to play games and it means that you're sinking to the same level as the person who is provoking you. Games use up the time you need for better things.

If you are hell-bent on getting your own back, then consider Marcus Aurelius: 'To refrain from imitation is the best revenge.'

Standing in front of a very angry person

Gandhi said, 'When you are right, you have no need to be angry. When you are wrong, you have no right to be angry.'

Wise words, but it's just possible that some of your colleagues, customers and managers will NOT share a deep understanding of the concept of self-control.

Anyone can get angry and anger is a normal and useful emotion. Unfortunately other people don't always manage their anger very well. (And ask yourself whether *you* do.)

There are some polite and effective ways to sidestep another person's anger when it's in your face and bordering on the abusive.

1. Think about offering some kind of assistance – something that may defuse the situation.

    For example, asking 'Are you OK?' or 'Is there anything I can do to help?' can have a rapid and surprisingly calming effect on someone if you get the tone right. It has to be sincere. (If they are angry with you personally, this won't work.) Can you offer them a place to talk? Would they like a cup of tea and a place to sit and talk it over? This gesture might sound lame but it has several things going for it. It allows you to think quickly while you're getting the tea. It tells the person that they have your time and attention and it may reduce the likelihood of upsetting other staff or customers. It also allows you to call for some kind of backup if you need it. And it's very hard to continue ranting and raving with a cup of tea in your hand.

2. Try saying 'Sorry' or 'You may be right.'

    If you are in the wrong, or partly in the wrong, you should say it anyway. Even if you're not, consider whether it's going to kill you to say 'sorry' for the situation that has arisen, or 'I'm sorry you feel that way.'

Again, watch your tone of voice and what your face is doing. If you say this while rolling your eyes and sighing loudly, it will antagonize the situation. Never swing out a hip, cross your arms, purse your lips and look at them as if they're an idiot – *even if they are behaving like an idiot.* You can always acknowledge an angry person's feelings. 'I can see that you're angry about that.' It doesn't mean you are agreeing with them or promising something you'll regret. It's better than standing there with your jaw open.

3. Ask a question to move the situation forward.
   Customer service professionals might ask, 'What do you want to see happen now?' Or 'What would fix this situation for you?' and that can be very useful at getting the person to calm down and think about what they actually want. Do they want an apology, a replacement, a refund or a repair? Any conversation that starts becoming more factual and focused on the future is going to lose angry steam. These questions move you forward from locking antlers and shouting.

4. Try to listen and stay calm.
   Obviously this goes against all our natural instincts to whack the person or run away. Naturally it feels embarrassing and threatening, and this increases if other people are listening in. But normal people do not become angry without a reason and if you can get them talking about this and try to solve the situation, or enlist some assistance, then they will calm down. It

may be a gradual reduction and time may be going unbearably slowly for you, but if you handle it well, you can find the angriest people apologizing and mumbling, 'Yeah, well, I know it's not your fault' and 'Sorry I lost it a bit there, but it's just not on, is it?' (and then looking very sheepish).

5. Let the small things go by.

   When people are angry they can throw out nasty, irrelevant taunts such as 'I want to speak to someone who can make a decision.' They can use insulting phrases like 'in the real world' as if you don't live in it, or start a sentence with 'The trouble with you people . . .' and then lump you together with every bad experience they've ever had.

   It's not fair or right and it can become completely unacceptable but try to let some of it go by. They are angry for a reason. Let them finish and blow out some steam so that you can hear the whole story and figure out the problem.

   If you bite on every word they say, or try to deal with every single taunt, you'll be there all day. Your goal at this point is not to defend your life or character, but to resolve this problem and get on with the day.

   It is not easy to cope with being provoked in this way. A hotel manager was recently telling me how infuriating it was to have an angry customer going over the top and their children chipping in with the same abusive language and angry gestures.

6. Don't make it worse.

A normal person's anger cannot last long without fuel. Like a toddler having a tantrum, their rage has to burn out at some point.

Fuel is having some small print quoted in a sneering, clipped voice.

Fuel is a lack of acknowledgement or being ignored. Having to repeat the problem all over again is infuriating, even for a calm person. The more a person has to repeat their problem, the angrier they will become. If you *know* you can't help them, then admit this to the person as soon as you can politely interrupt. Go for help but first tell the person that you are going to fetch a certain person for them – if they would kindly wait. Or tell them that that person will call them back or contact them. (And make sure that promise happens or else their anger will start becoming personal.)

Fuel is also being insulting, rude or sarcastic in return. In a bank recently, I heard an elderly woman ask a uniformed staff member why the queue for the tellers was so long. She was leaning on her walking stick and had, like me, come in early to avoid a busy branch. 'I know, I know,' said the trainee manager, shaking her head with a sigh, 'but until *you* people learn to use the ATMs and stop lining up like sheep for every simple transaction, I don't see what we can do.' That's what I would call fuel. And not only was the elderly woman furious, but every other customer in the line turned to glare and snort at the manager.

7. Never, ever join in.

   If people cross a line, then signal for help. It's OK to warn people that they are out of order. 'If you continue to speak to me in this way, I will have to ask you to leave' or 'I can help you when you have calmed down.'

   Spell out the consequences and, if absolutely necessary, be prepared to walk away. (Keep walking in spite of whatever they say as you leave.)

   It is also possible to have completely irrational people wander into your workplace. Shops, in particular, are quite vulnerable and people who work with the general public can be very exposed.

   Managers need to make judgement calls without the benefit of a psychiatric qualification, but, invariably, businesses attract a few regular 'characters' and someone should know how to handle the situation.

   Customers and employees can lash out in anger. But work is not a sandpit with your mother saying, 'Well, hit him back then!' You should defend yourself – absolutely – but never do anything aggressive in return. Medical insurance might not be forthcoming if you contributed to the problem in any way. If an employee hits you in the workplace, then it's instant dismissal for them. If a customer hits you, it's called assault. Let your employer or the police deal with them. Learn to defend yourself safely and if your workplace is such that attacks could occur, then ask in advance for advice for handling these situations.

8. Put the fire out.

If you've stood in front of anger and abuse and you feel upset, then don't be embarrassed about that. It's not unusual to shake a bit, burst into tears or feel quite shocked. It shows that your natural defences are working if your heart rate is up and you feel a bit flustered. Talk it over, go for a walk and don't be afraid to stop and think about it. In the long term we can all use some kind of outlet for the built-up distress that everyday situations can produce.

But whatever you do, don't spread it around. Don't snap at the next person you see! Misery and anger are as contagious as enthusiasm and good manners. Nip it in the bud.

**‘‘Life is mostly froth and bubble,
Two things stand like stone,
Kindness in another's trouble
Courage in your own.’’**

Adam Lindsay Gordon

Dealing with bizarre behaviour

There is behaviour that falls into a category of its own. It is the kind of habit or action that becomes infamous and almost legend in the office gossip. It can also be irritating, revolting or just disturbing in a creepy way. I get to hear such a variety of 'people problems' that I could list pages' worth but here's a small sample of the kinds of anti-social behaviour that come to work and cause distress:

- A secretary who spends an hour each morning squeezing, tweezing, filing nails and (for an encore) shaking her dandruff onto the desk

- The manager who deliberately calls meetings at a time of day when she knows a working mum cannot be there

- An employee who keeps a notebook on another colleague's every move

- A manager who always asks (about female job candidates) 'has she got big tits?'

- An employee who is in charge of the stores and makes everyone go through ridiculous hurdles to get their supplies. He then tells people to come for their orders within a ten minute window each day

- A manager who goes into somewhat disturbing detail about the women that he dates

- A female employee who goes into similarly gruesome detail about her experiences of childbirth and her children's illnesses

I could go on but you get the drift. This behaviour shows such poor self-awareness or thought for others that it is often avoided as an issue to be addressed. The manager concerned does not know where to start.

But the options are the same as for every difficult situation.

> Is it a real problem affecting work?
> What do you want to do about it?
> You can do something about it or rise above it.

If the behaviour crosses a line, you may need to get other people (such as security, personnel or a senior manager) to help or advise you.

Keeping things in proportion

It's a cliché, but *mud sticks*. We're fairly good at remembering awful things. We can easily become obsessive about something negative that's going on. We can loathe our work because of someone's behaviour, forgetting all the other 'easygoing' people. We can think of a person only in terms of the problem that we observe. We can fester instead of getting on with our work or looking forward. We can fail to credit someone with making a positive change in his or her behaviour.

In our reactions, we can become overly aggressive, avoid important things, spend too much time dreaming of escape or lose concentration as fight/flight responses to our distress.

We might go to great lengths to avoid having to speak to these people, sit in a meeting or work with them.

I've done it. I have allowed myself to become ill over 'problems' and I have lain awake, angry and upset about other people's behaviour. I have wondered how someone could tell a blatant lie or be such a coward. It was, and is, pointless speculation. Few people ever admit to these traits and often, in their own minds, there has been no transgression.

In terms of perspective, if I think about the thousands of people I've encountered through work, there were maybe half a dozen people in total that actually disturbed me in this way. And all this angst was a complete waste of my energy, my time and therefore my life.

We might have exceptional skills when we get to work, but they're unlikely to be enough to help us love our work. Unless and until we manage our own behaviour and improve the ways in which we deal with other people, there is the potential for problems. These may be serious enough to make us loathe our work.

We always have a 'get out of jail' card available if we get it wrong. If we misunderstand or fail to behave as we could have, and if we want to fix things, we can always say 'sorry'. No one's perfect all the time. (That would be too boring for words.)

You can start again with people if there's a will on both sides to move forward. I've seen it happen many times.

The bad news is there are no guarantees. You may do all the right things and employ a logical strategy in trying to deal with a conflict situation. There is no guarantee that you will get the desired outcome. We cannot control or predict other people's behaviour. At best, we can influence it. Still, that's pretty useful and always worth trying.

We're always going to have conflicts because we're always going to work with some people who see things differently. It is pointless to wish for a place in the world where everyone agrees with you all of the time. It wouldn't be a healthy place to be in, since constructive conflict and differences help us avoid the dangers of narrow-mindedness and lead us toward growth and innovation.

Working with other people can and should add to our lives rather than subtract from them if we can only learn to work with differences rather than wasting time in obstruction and anger.

CHAPTER 7

CHANGE THE WORK YOU DO

If it's the wrong job, how do you find the right one?

"It's never too late to be what you might have been."

George Eliot

After ten years in law you realize you always wanted to be in radio. After ten years in radio you realize you always wanted to be in law. I have recently met two former Olympic athletes who are working on construction sites. They could be in the sports world but they want to be out building things. It's OK. We don't start out at fifteen with a perfect view of the career that will always be right for us. And what feels 'right' for us at one point in our lives may simply not fit us later on. Who is to say that we should have one career or skill in our lifetime?

If you cannot abide the idea of being in the same career for the next ten years, then it may be a very good time to plan for the career that you would like to be in. Of course, it's tough to sit in classes with people much younger than you or find yourself delivering the post around a new office, because that's the job that the new people do. It's hard to start at the bottom if you've left security and perks and status somewhere behind you. But people do this. Ask yourself, would that be so terrible and would it be worse than staying where you are for another ten years?

You might make an attractive starter to an employer. You already have work experience. You might bring in some knowledge and experience, even if it seems completely unrelated. Employers always hope and assume that older starters have some wisdom and maturity and a basic work ethic in place, such as knowing that you have to show up on time and some common sense and ease in dealing with customers. People who come to an employer asking for work, with a desire to do something they have long wanted to do, are appealing recruits to a smart boss. You cannot buy passion and enthusiasm, and it's great when it comes straight to your door. What you cannot expect is to keep your existing salary. (See 'downshifting', page 186). You may have to start where every junior starts. You have to learn and listen. You do have to show a willingness to do the grungy tasks. Your employer may have some concerns about whether you have energy and enthusiasm and an ability to be open-minded. How will you prove to someone that you're serious about this change? Have you enrolled in some related course? Have you been following what's happening in this new industry or business? What are you investing of yourself in this? In short, is this a mid-life crisis or are you sincere about a new start?

Is it a wobble or a real desire for change? Are you just certain that you don't want the existing job anymore? *And have you thought through what you really want to do instead?* What if you're not sure?

How to decide what you really want to do

If you were searching for the 'right' person to spend the rest of your life with, what criteria would you use to guide you? Sometimes our relationship with work lasts longer than a personal relationship, so I use this comparison deliberately. Finding work that is right for you is an important search, but it's not a simple one. There's no arcade machine or twenty-question quiz that produces the magic solution.

It's easy to feel stumped unless you have a useful set of questions as a guide. Anyone can blunder into that dead zone in careers called 'I DUNNO – I DIDN'T REALLY THINK ABOUT IT'.

The *worst* questions for making big decisions about your working life are these:

> What jobs are on offer around here?
> What are all my friends doing?
> What pays more?
> What are the easiest hours?
> What do my parents do?
> What kind of job has the longest holidays?
> Who has the best canteen?
> What kind of job would make me look cool?

These questions are not likely to lead you to work satisfaction.

The *better* questions take time and thought, and if you want to find work that's right for you, then *make that time.*

1. If I could do anything with my life, what would that be? Spend some real time dreaming – as if there were no barriers. You might have some broad ideas about what you want to do. For example, you may want to do something:

Arty
Outdoors
Involving technical skills
In retail

In the caring professions

To do with computers

In media or music

In the medical field

Involving design

Involving travel

Where you can meet a lot of people

That requires problem-solving

That lets you work in peace and quiet

Around aircraft

To do with farming or agriculture

To do with large companies

And so on . . .

This isn't an either/or game. You may have more than one area of interest. Always ask yourself *why* after every statement. WHY do you wish to travel? WHY are you attracted to the caring professions? WHY wouldn't you want to do something in computers?

2. What would I attempt to do if I knew I could not fail? This question, from Dr Robert Schuller, is a terrific prompt for dreaming. A fear of failure and self-doubt can hold us back from simply naming a goal or ambition.

3. What kinds of activities, interests or tasks do I get a real kick out of?
    What is it about that hobby that holds your interest? When you have free time, what do you choose to do? When you have spare cash, what do you spend it on? What kinds of things are you happy to help others

with? What requests for help sound like a drag? What kind of work would you do for free? If you were incredibly rich, what kind of work would you do just for your interest's sake?

4. What *kind* of life do I want to live?

    Do you have any lifestyle goals? Do you want to switch off easily when the work is done? Do you want work that involves you in a community? Do you want a career that leads you, more easily, into another arena – like politics?

5. What do I do well?

    Competence matters. The things you're good at might be difficult for you to see or appreciate. Can you ask other people, particularly someone with a lot of life experience for some clues? Tell them you're not fishing for compliments – you're trying to find out about any talents or qualities that they observe in you. These may be intangible skills, like being a good finisher, a good organizer, being calm with people or having a rare sense of humour.

> **"There once was a man who said "Damn,**
> **At last I've found out what I am**
> **A creature that moves**
> **In predestinate grooves**
> **I'm not even a bus, I'm a tram!"**
>
> *Maurice E. Hare*

6. Who do I think has a really satisfying or rewarding *working* life?

    What is it about that person's working life that appeals to you? And conversely, is there anyone whose working life makes you think 'I don't want to end up like that!' (I was mildly terrified of starting and finishing work at exactly the same time each day. Other people are terrified of jobs with erratic hours.)

7. What kinds of people do I enjoy being around?
   Who inspires you to do better? Who makes you feel enthusiastic?

   Who makes you feel angry, irritable or vaguely depressed and why is that so? This will give you some clues about the kind of work environment that might suit you.

8. What kinds of behaviours in others do I find acceptable/unacceptable?
   If you feel you could not work with extreme rudeness, you may not be suited to customer service work. If you have very strong views on how people should live, you might find social work a bit of a challenge.

   It's worth talking this through with someone who knows you well.

9. What kind of career would be a fair exchange for years of my time and energy?
   Try to imagine yourself at 80. Now – imagine you are looking back on your working life. Can you get any sense for the kind of working life that you'd feel satisfied with? Do you think there's a life you might regret? I tried this and got a picture of myself regretting not working for myself. I felt I'd regret staying in one place or in one company for too long. I felt I would like to

have done something different, perhaps something very new rather than a traditional occupation. I knew that I'd want to have mixed with very different kinds of people.

And finally:

10. What did I say I wanted to do when I was a child? What did I say I'd do before I reached an age where I told myself I couldn't? We're never too old to revisit this question. It *may* still be relevant, particularly if you hung on to that answer for a long time. Some of the happiest and most capable people I have met have told me that they're doing something that *they always wanted to do – for as long as they could recall.*

These questions are often pushed aside when we don't have the confidence or belief in ourselves to follow our own hopes and dreams.

To love your work, you have to get your choice of work very close to YOU. You cannot take someone else's answers and make them work for you.

If you can get a feeling, even a vague feeling, for what you want to do, then **you can find out more**. As you know more, **you can plan**. A plan is a good start. It is not written in stone. A plan can change and you might never follow it exactly, but it will be there to remind you of your overall aspirations.

Seek advice but sift it carefully

You need useful information about **work** and realistic information about **yourself**, because you need to marry the two. But judge the advice you get very carefully. You need to weigh up the views of people whose opinions you might have always *accepted* without question. You may want to reconsider comments you have always *rejected* without question.

And if you are 'among the very young at heart', then this might be difficult. Confusion reigns. You might receive friendly and persistent advice from people who are out of touch with current employment trends and requirements.

One of my older relatives encouraged me to work in a company that gave the 'girls' a uniform, had a good canteen and 'a marvellous hosiery allowance!' (She was being kind.) I was advised by more than one person to do something for fun after I left school. 'You'll be giving it up once you're married anyway.' (Careless and disturbing advice, assuming I would never need to work or be financially independent beyond a wedding day.)

One of my school teachers encouraged me to join her profession. 'The holidays are brilliant and you can always get an instant loan through the Teachers Credit Union.'

The career guidance teacher assigned to my high school was a rare sight. On one of the occasions that she deigned to visit, we were handed a pamphlet with a list of possible occupations from A to Z. It began with Actuary and ended with Zoologist. (It was about as helpful as visiting a travel agent and being handed an atlas.)

When you've been working, you have the opportunity to ask colleagues (and former workmates) what skills and tasks *they* think suited you. They might easily recall the kinds of things you preferred to avoid, especially if you always left it for them to do!

Friends can chip in with advice but it may not always be constructive. Having a passion for gardening does not necessarily mean you should go into landscaping. Being able to throw a good dinner party does not mean you will be suited to running a restaurant. Owning every series of *ER* does not mean you belong in a casualty team. It's warm and fuzzy to suggest, as magazines and some hyper-motivation books are wont to do, that you should go for that dream job but it does not necessarily follow that you're cut out for it. It doesn't sound terribly exciting, but what about organizing some kind of work experience? At the very least, talk and *listen* to people who work in those jobs. Not only may they give you invaluable information but, if the job doesn't seem right for you, save you from disappointment and a waste of time.

Labels can be lifelong shackles.

> 'Oh, we always said you'd be running the country before you were 21.'
> 'You're just a born secretary.'
> 'I always knew you weren't cut out for hard work.'

Try to tune out this kind of talk when you're thinking about what you want to do.

Sometimes other people try to help by advising you to go into a career that made *them* happy. That's well intended but not necessarily helpful, although it's always good to hear people speak positively about their working lives. You might ask them *why* their career made them happy.

You need advice and information, but *sift it carefully.*

Looking for work

Don't wait to see your dream job appear in the paper. Work is more commonly found by a **direct approach** to employers or through **contacts**.

With a plan you can ask people to help you. You can find the person who knows 'how you get into this kind of work'. **Be politely persistent** for information and addresses. Ask a friendly librarian for help in your search for information. (They're usually brilliant at this.) Use the Internet. Make phone calls. Knock on doors. Use whatever means you can.

Whatever craft, profession or trade you're interested in, whether it is accounting, cooking, engineering, picture framing or truck driving, *usually* has some association, guild or information service. Get the number and ask for careers advice or a list of members. Industries and trades tend to club together for lots of reasons, but one useful reason is to provide information to people coming in.

To repeat a suggestion, is there any possibility for some kind of work experience?

Work experience is not only for school students. Can you take a look at what that job is REALLY like, even for a short time? This strategy saved me from three different professions which would not have suited me at all.

Ask someone who is in the workforce to show you a good CV, or at least to check your draft effort and make comments. Certainly ask someone to check the spelling. Silly mistakes tend to leap off the page and may be a "good enough" reason for a harassed recruiter to reject your application.

In my own experience, I have become very wary of agencies and their capacity to match me with work that I am capable of doing and enjoying. Even so, they *are* sources of work and can link you to opportunities.

Of course, the newspaper is still a source of work but get hold of *all* the relevant papers and journals that carry the vacancies you're looking for. It's worth asking the local news seller for relevant magazines and papers. And the library, again, is a good place to ask for help. You don't have to buy papers and magazines if the library stocks them and has a photocopier. And people are likely to share their copies if they know what you're doing.

There's also the possibility of advertising *your skills* under situations wanted – on notice boards or in papers. You can design an advertisement, or get some help to do this, and send it through doors or the appropriate letterboxes.

A good friend became a theatre critic for a newspaper. I asked him how he got the job.

'You just write some sample reviews and send them around. Of course you have to keep at the editors and persist.' (And there was me, thinking that he had applied for a job opening as 'critic' and interviewed successfully!)

I read a story about a British teenager going off to do work experience at NASA. He was asked the same question that I asked my critic friend, 'How did you get such a placement?'

'My mum wrote off and asked them,' he said.

Don't be afraid to ask people for help, try out for work experience and risk rejection by applying directly to employers. Don't be afraid to ask (politely) for fifteen minutes of someone's time. It's not a guarantee that doors will open, but it's surprising how often they do.

The worst you might ever hear is 'NO' and even then, it's usually 'NO, not at this moment, but maybe some time in the future.' And you can live with 'no'. It's not a fatal wound.

"Life shrinks or expands in proportion to one's courage."

Anaïs Nin

Apathy, ignorance and 'not got around to it yet' are the biggest enemies in the job search business. I've worked with women who spend hundreds of hours planning their wedding day but think it's quite acceptable to have never put an hour into career planning for life. (But it is, apparently, quite acceptable to complain about 'never getting anywhere'.)

I've worked with colleagues who will put more effort and thought into planning a holiday or buying a new car than they're prepared to invest in finding employment that will fulfil their potential and possibly help them to be happier people. To buy a new car, they are prepared to visit motor shows, watch car review programmes, pick up car magazines, visit car showrooms and tell everyone to look out for them before making a choice.

For their career – that 'thing' that takes up such an enormous chunk of their lives – some of these people are prepared to wait until they see an opportunity in front of their noses. They may glance at the one notice board they can be bothered to look at or skim the free classifieds of a poor quality paper. For the sake of a few phone calls, stamps, envelopes, copies of other newspapers, trips to the local library or a visit to a new notice board, a lot of people will miss out on interesting work or give up searching for it. If they don't see a specific job advertised that they can apply for, then they believe that jobs are too hard to come by. If they get rejected once, they believe it's forever. (And then it is easy to blame outside factors for the lacklustre state of their working lives.)

There is no shame in asking around, leaving your name and number with the hiring person or chasing up a call or letter that hasn't been answered. Do all this with good manners and basic courtesy. This is not about luck; *it's about persistence.*

'Fortune favours the brave' and the job search process is much kinder to people who are prepared to keep trying, wear out some shoe leather and persist with their calls and applications.

Handling the downside of looking for work

Rejection

If you're in a job, the time spent searching for what you *really* want could easily fly by. You're occupied and earning. But if you're between jobs or still in the wrong job and trying hard to get a new break, you can go through some slumpy, bumpy moments when your morale is low and you start to wonder if it's worth it.

Something to bear in mind when you receive another 'no' letter is that recruitment is not a process of selection. *It is a process of rejection.* With a pile of papers in front of them, employers will sift people *out* until they arrive at the details which best match the role (as they see it) and raise the least number of concerns. They may draw up a shortlist of people that they believe seem close enough. It is not a perfect science and unfair decisions can so easily be made.

It still hurts (a bit) to get a reject letter when you made it to the interview stage. It hurts even more to get a reject letter when you were sure you had the job or made it to a third round. (I got the 'sorry' call once when I'd been given the job at the interview.)

But hang on! If you made it to the interview stage, congratulate yourself! Is there a chance to be considered in the future if you were close? ASK THEM.

It's woeful when you don't get an answer to a letter or a return phone call at all. You'll know better when you're in the same position one day. ALWAYS acknowledge people.

Friendly interest

Sometimes 'friendly' interest can drive you mad. Unhelpful questions and comments come at you – such as,

- 'What do you do with yourself all day?' (from someone who spends their day watching soaps)

- 'But there's plenty of jobs up at the shoe factory' (when you're a research chemist)

- 'But Cousin Eddie got a job without any trouble' (when Cousin Eddie frightens Doberman dogs)

- 'Well you're obviously not trying your best' (when you are)

- 'Why haven't you found something yet?' (as if there's something desperately wrong with you)

- 'When I was your age . . .' (from someone who last worked in the days before electricity)

- Even a simple 'How's the job hunting going?' can depress you when you're trying to cope with a bad slump.

'Friendly' interest is annoying at times, but think of the alternative; no one giving a damn. Rather than the obvious tactic of withdrawing and avoiding people (which is not good for you), try asserting yourself politely and saying 'OK. Thanks for asking' and then change the subject. If necessary, ask 'Can we talk about something else?'

If they ignore you and persist, you have every reason to avoid that person or draw attention to their tactless behaviour. (Or just ask if Cousin Eddie is still enjoying the job his probation officer found for him.)

Occasional slumps

More worrying is the way you speak to yourself. Anyone can let in the creeping fear that 'this goal will never be achieved'. When you observe how others compromise on their lives, you can wonder, 'Am I kidding myself to have this goal?' The question 'Who do you think you are?' starts echoing in the conscious mind.

Worse is the fear that you might never work again. Confident and capable people can experience these fears. You might start to look at the hurrying masses as they head for the bus stop and wonder if you'll ever join them again. Losing your nerve and talking yourself out of even trying is another big gremlin to watch out for.

How can we persist when we want to crawl away?

Don't let rejection get to you personally. It *feels* personal but of course it isn't. How can it be personal when the recruiter doesn't know you? Treat every rejection as a learning opportunity and one step closer to the YES letter or call.

I read about an Oscar-nominated screenwriter who papered his study walls with reject letters. Do that! Keep hold of those letters in a file called 'One day I'll look back and laugh'.

I once missed out on a job that I really wanted. I was hugely disappointed, but more so when I discovered the Managing Director had given the job to his daughter's boyfriend. Within a few years I had the opportunity to write both daughter AND boyfriend reject letters. It's a small world. The letters were polite and genuine. There really wasn't a job for either of them, but I confess I signed my name with a flourish. (OK, I admit to whistling as I dropped those letters in the out tray.)

Keep yourself active mentally and physically. Have you been meaning to fix the garden, sort out old photos, tidy out a spare room or help someone you know? Is there a huge novel you always meant to read? Adult classes are often inexpensive. Walking is free, and so are a lot of museums and galleries. What's happening near you? Get some sense of achievement.

"The cure for this ill is not to sit still,
Or frowst with a book by the fire;
But to take a large hoe and shovel also,
And dig til you gently perspire;"

Rudyard Kipling

Think of your work search as a project. Keep a file or spreadsheet on the go. Track how letters and calls are going so that every day you have a list of things to do to move this project along. Do this at a certain time each day when your energy and enthusiasm are up. And when you're done with writing,

Think of your work search as a project.

phoning, replying and whatever else, write an updated list of 'things to do' tomorrow and take a break from it. Go for a walk. Go for a coffee. Read your favourite things. Watch a favourite movie. Treat yourself.

Keep talking to your network. Don't drop out of sight, or people will assume you found what you wanted. You might want to crawl away sometimes but please don't. Tell people what you're doing and what you're looking for so they can keep an eye out for you.

If you're bored or frustrated and would do anything to pass the time, then tell people that too. You never know what might come your way. I was once offered some work in a bookstore to help 'pass the time'. It was wonderful. You can never be sure that this 'time passing' won't lead to some useful knowledge or contacts.

Because you're following your hopes, the people who really care about you do not think you're a loser. They might, however, let this word drift across their minds if you give up completely and make a permanent dent in the sofa. They may be disappointed if you spend the next twenty years complaining because you hate what you do. Don't let the word 'loser' into your head when you're searching.

If you've hit a rough patch, tell someone you trust so they can make you laugh. Keep close to **people who are positive** and supportive. Avoid the ones who pull you down.

Keep **a balance in your life**. Remember to **have a life**. Other chores still need your attention. Get ready for the day, as you always did.

When you set a goal high you may fall a bit short – but that's OK. Employers might say, 'There's nothing right now but in six months time there might be, so stay in touch.' *Or* 'We don't have that exact opportunity, but what about this?' It may help to be on the spot when the next 'opportunity' becomes free.

Remember this too: Very few people walk straight into their 'dream work'. Persistence is everything. There are detours and diversions along the way.

"No great thing is created suddenly."

Epictetus

New skills or qualifications – going back to the books

In my first year of college I met a boy who had found, after two years of law, that he didn't see any future in it for himself. He began to dread every class and couldn't remember why he'd ever chosen to study it. He came to the painful decision to change *now* or pursue a career he knew he'd never be happy in.

I recall saying (with all the tact and wisdom of an eighteen-year-old) that 'I wouldn't be able to live with myself if I'd wasted all that time.' Of course, the real sadness would have been for him to continue on in his state of misery. Only a fool persists with an obvious mistake.

I also failed to see the fact that the combination of his studies actually made him very employable. (I must add that his family supported him through the change in direction. It was also his good fortune that his parents valued their son's happiness and peace of mind. That is not always the case.)

You *can* change direction. You *can* go back and study. You are free to change your mind at 16, 26, 36, 46 and so on. It may take a lot of organizing and sacrifice, but it *can* be done. Of course, it may not be an easy thing to do but it is not an impossible thing to do.

It is easier to do when you're prepared and able to downshift financially, but even this may not be necessary. You might continue with your work and study part-time or do something called 'block release', which means studying for set weeks at a time. Many colleges and universities offer distance learning, which has been made even more accessible through the Internet.

By the time I finished my degree (part-time and in the evenings after work) my classes were full of working people. Some had jobs *and* young families. I don't know how they juggled their lives but I tip my hat to them.

Sometimes people tell me that part-time study is 'impossible'. I have to disagree when this is said by someone who regularly props up a bar or watches hours of mindless TV every day. Combining work and study is certainly hard work, but it is *not* unrealistic.

"When people say to me: 'How do you do so many things?' I often answer them, without meaning to be cruel: 'How do you do so little?'

It seems to me that people have vast potential. Most people can do extraordinary things if they have the confidence or take the risks. Yet most people don't. They sit in front of the telly and treat life as if it goes on forever."

Phillip Adams

Downshifting is an option

Downshifting (also known as 'voluntary simplicity') is a new term for an old feeling. It just means 'I don't want this working life any more.' It's no longer a euphemism for early retirement – growing numbers of people who are many years from retirement age are doing this.

Frequently it means cutting your working hours and pay (and probably your career prospects) for more free time. When you downshift you trade your existing work situation (and the money that goes with it) for something else. That 'something else' may be study, stopping work, taking a gap year, starting over, volunteering, going part-time, going freelance or starting your own business. It may be that you simply want more time for hobbies, children or time to breathe. It can mean opting out altogether but it can also involve staying with the same employer and just reducing your working week.

It's a good option if you are at a point where you value time more than money and you're confident about living on a reduced income. Downshifting is not a good idea if you need every penny you earn or you still feel ambitious (even just a bit) in your field of work.

How do you downshift?

A useful first step is to go through your finances with great care. Can you live on less? How much do you need, honestly? Be very realistic with your sums. Reducing your working hours means that you automatically drop associated costs such as commuting, work clothes, lunches, convenience foods, dry cleaning, childcare, parking and the social life that goes with work, from chipping in for presents to buying rounds at the pub.

Try to live on the reduced income for a few months and see how you cope. (Are you sure you can live without the odd splurge?)

Having dealt with debt and learned to live on less, successful downshifters usually have a cash reserve. In fact, a reserve for emergencies is a good idea for anyone who wants to study, take time out, change to a lesser paid career or start a small business. It reduces some of the anxiety. (About three to six months' salary is a good idea.)

There are reasons why downshifters struggle and it's not all to do with the drop in money. There are aspects to work that we only appreciate when work, as we knew it, is gone. Work provides a social life. It provides contact with human beings. It provides mental stimulation – well, most of it does!

Work provides a certain amount of status. People ask, 'What do you do?' in social settings and most of us are uncomfortable answering, 'Not much if I can help it.' Can you cope with people describing you as having 'dropped out' or 'quit the fast lane'?

The status aspect of work hits us in more ways than one. Do you mind if someone who started years after you did is promoted to the job you wanted? Do you mind if colleagues make a mess of the work you had done? Is it OK if they throw away something that mattered to you or decide to do something you fought against? Are you genuinely ready to leave?

Do you want to work for yourself?

If you want to go out on your own by starting a business or freelancing in what you already do, then plan the move carefully. (If it never occurred to you to be self-employed or to run a business until you read that sentence, then this is not a good option.) You need vast amounts of self-motivation to succeed and the entrepreneurial spirit does not suddenly emerge in someone who is a bit cheesed off with work and thinks 'might as well give it a go'.

There can be a great feeling of pride (an old-fashioned notion but it's still about) in saying 'I work for myself.' Small businesses are an important part of the communities they exist in. Small business owners and the self-employed have (and need) very good networks. The constant stimulation – of facing the customer and the product, of keeping a business going successfully and keeping it solvent – is something that many people thrive on and would never leave.

Starting a new business

A critical first step (again) is to get some sound advice. The statistics on small business start-ups are not encouraging but the causes of failure are all too common, from going into something you know nothing about to going into business with people who let you down. Probably the biggest killer of start-ups is cash flow. You may have a great idea and loads of talent and energy but if you don't understand money and how you will spend it and collect it – your dream could be over very quickly.

Find out all the gritty, boring aspects of running any business, from legal requirements to cash flow, before you set off and while you're earning some money. If you don't have the patience to do that, then consider very carefully whether you will cope with the responsibility of being on your own. The paperwork does not go away. There are books out there that will help and government bodies that offer good advice on the Internet. Find out as much as you can about the kind of business you want to go into and make some contacts now if you possibly can.

Go and work in this kind of business, even if you have to work on your weekends. Take great care about going into business with other people, even if you're related to them. Plan and prepare before you put up your house for a business loan.

Going freelance

A 'free lance' was a 'lance' or knight for hire. So when the term *mercenary* is flung at a consultant, it's not so far from the truth. Few freelancers today carry sharpened weapons and even fewer travel by steed, but outsourcing, downsizing, home-working and the end of the 'jobs for life' era have all seen a big rise in freelancing. Home computers and mobile phones have also made freelancing terribly easy.

Freelancing can be much less expensive than starting a small business. The overheads for a freelancer may simply be a small workspace at home, a phone, some business cards, letterhead, computer and a few decent contacts for work.

You might be ready for freelancing if you really enjoy your profession or skill but want to work for yourself. There is still that satisfaction in saying 'I work for myself.' There is more freedom although it is not absolute freedom. You still have to make a living and can find yourself saying 'yes' to work that you'd rather not do. You have to go and find your work. If you don't like 'selling' yourself it's going to be harder for you. (Not impossible, but you'll have to gird up your loins from time to time!)

I have been freelancing for a while and one of the greatest perks, in my opinion, is working in such different industries and businesses. This means that I am constantly learning and I like that. I like saying that I'm the managing director of a small company. Of course, I am also the tea lady and the filing clerk, but that's another matter.

Freelancers charge more per day than salaried workers, but this is balanced out by the fact that there is no paid leave or other benefits. A sick day is a day of lost earnings and, potentially, a lost client. Freelancers can escape a lot of office politics, but you never escape it entirely because where there are human beings there is politics. And as with starting a small business, you need a very high degree of self-motivation and the willingness to tackle the paperwork. The taxman hasn't lost sight of you just because you left a payroll. The same financial concerns are there and that cash reserve is still a good idea. People might pay slowly. Some may not pay at all. Could you handle an empty stretch? As one freelancer said to me before I made the leap, 'When the diary's full, it's a wonderful feeling. You wonder why anyone would trade this life in. But when the diary is empty and you see weeks without work and blank pages, you think oh ****! What have I done?'

The big question is whether you have reached a level of skill and competence that allows you to sell your skill. It's an important question and worth getting very straightforward advice on. You will be up against serious competition for work.

Maybe you just need a good break

If you really need a change and just cannot think of alternatives, then maybe a good break from everything would help you think it through. It's possibly not your job that is getting you down. You might be tired and a few months are all that's needed to get back some focus and think through your options.

Sabbaticals, family leave, gap years and leave without pay are all options worth talking about. (Who said you had to be a school leaver to take a gap year?)

Workplaces are loosening up about this kind of thing and *flexibility* is a big word in many large companies. There is greater awareness of genuine stress. Taking time out is far better than becoming ill, walking out the front door and burning your bridges or doing something desperate because you're at breaking point.

Agreeing this (and please don't make the mistake of demanding it) ensures you've got something to come back to. You may decide you don't want to come back but that's OK. You've got time to think about it. Maybe you'll come back to it with renewed motivation and some colour in your cheeks. It's a good idea to do something with that time. Travel the world, fix the garden or just do whatever would give you back some perspective. Sitting in front of daytime TV is not going to make you feel better.

Detours along the way

What do you do for a living?

I can think of very few friends and colleagues who can easily and neatly describe their work. Some of them do not have titles. Some have careers that are so specialized that nobody understands what they do even if they *try* to explain it. Some have careers that are a curious blend of things that they find interesting. Some have been able to get other people to buy their time, skills or ideas. Very few have stayed in the profession or work area that they first joined but invariably they have found a way to use that experience as a building block for the later choices.

There are side paths and detours along the way to finding work that you love. There may be temporary or part-time jobs that you take which don't form part of your plan and certainly fall outside your aspirations. Amongst the jobs that I (and my friends) have done are burger flipping, hospital cleaning, shovel wielding, filing, dishwashing, factory work, shop assisting, bartending, debt collecting, phone answering, babysitting and calling out 'May I take your order please?'

In some of my detour jobs I met people who had been doing the same task for a long time and they *weren't* passing through. Some of these people were happy. It was what they wanted to do. Some were not happy. Some were festering. Some were serial whiners, locked into irrational beliefs about why they were 'trapped'. They could occasionally be destructive co-workers. But you needn't join them or share their attitude.

Don't get despondent. You can always learn something and there can be hidden treasures in some of these detour jobs. One friend has enrolled in nursing after the detour job in a hospital made her realize, '*This* is what I want to do.' She's now a mature student in a nursing degree. This revelation came after about 15 years of working in unsatisfying office jobs.

Another friend went into hospitality and hotel management. She had observed, as a part-time waitress for large weddings and banquets, that large hotels were interesting places. The same hotel gave her a permanent start at reception and within a short time she was the front office manager.

Most of my friends and colleagues have taken time out or changed direction at some point. You *can* try out other things. It won't necessarily leave a terrible stain on your CV unless you flit around for years and show no sign of committing to anything.

Do what you love – love what you do

Don't get sucked into believing that you have to wear a suit, be busy every minute of your life or get a promotion every year. I hope that you have the self-confidence to pursue the work you think you'll love, in spite of the pressures to conform or aspire in other directions. The inability to hold on to our own dreams probably accounts for the fact that too many 'successful' people feel acute stress, suffer burnout or become martyrs to work that they cannot love.

When I first started reading and learning about careers and self-esteem, much of the material IMPLIED that we should all want promotion. Promotion was the necessary stamp to indicate that you had done well.

Success was frequently portrayed as excess. There was little discussion about the wide variety of goals that people might have. The person who said 'I want to make enough money and have the time to pursue my love of windsurfing' was not playing the game. Success was certainly beautiful and ambitious. Success was invariably about money. (Who am I kidding? Success still IS about money for many people.)

But what I found, in the land of suits and swinging briefcases, was a lot of 'successful' people who felt disenchanted, tired and unfulfilled. Some would say, 'You, too, can "have it all" and here, take my ulcer while you're at it!'

There's another side to this 'glamorous' successful world that I was being tempted with, and I heard some confess, 'I put my life into a job that I didn't love and I missed out on seeing my kids grow up. Don't I feel like a fool? I can never get those years back now. They gave me a golden handshake. It wasn't worth it.'

There was very little in the 'success' literature about accepting yourself and your own ambitions **or lack of them**.

What if you want to be a landscape gardener? You won't be wearing suits. You might swing a shovel instead of a briefcase. You'll have callused, rather than manicured, hands. The financial returns aren't great and the prospects for promotion barely exist. Or it might be that you love tinkering with engines all day, or love to teach or love to drive a truck. If you know what you love to do and can make a living out of it, isn't that success?

Perhaps we'd better start to think so. Careers have changed a bit. The workplace has changed a bit. 'Rapid and unprecedented change' is a phrase that I hear often.

The loss of job security and the enormous changes going on inside organizations mean that anyone with a very fixed view on how they'll **always** make a living may be in for a shock.

My friend Kate is not remotely ambitious for promotion. She doesn't set goals and admits this freely, but she does take responsibility for her life and her career choices. She'll accept opportunities to vary the work if these come her way. Kate's talents lie in clear thinking, organizing and handling people in difficult situations. She has a robust self-image and a sense of humour that attracts everyone. She's a highly valued and capable employee. Kate *loves* her work.

We have a carpenter called Joe, who is reliable and friendly. Joe *also* loves his work, building something that is solid and well crafted out of wood. When the job is finished, he takes genuine pride in the end result, sometimes bringing family around to view the finished project. Joe had learning difficulties as a child and was never singled out as being particularly brilliant, but he's in huge demand. His diary is full. He has the freedom to say 'no' to work that he doesn't want to do.

In a temporary job for a medical supplies company (years ago) I met Douglas. He also loved his work. Douglas knew the name of every customer and answered his phone with huge outbursts of enthusiasm that made me laugh. He remembered little things about his customers, like children's names and whether they'd finished having their house painted yet. He took an interest in people and the products he was supplying. His knowledge was extraordinary. If he was away, the place seemed incredibly flat. How easily he could have carried out the same job without the fun. In terms of customer relationships and getting loyalty for the business, he was an absolute star. Yet he's not what most people would imagine when they think of a top salesman. Douglas also liked to knit and wore his multicoloured creations to work. I couldn't see him in a suit.

When I think of the word *success*, I think of people like Douglas and Kate and Joe. I have stopped picturing the Porsche and the share trading floor and the expense account long ago. Kate, Joe and Douglas are people who love their work and yet would not necessarily be described at their school reunions as being highly successful. I'm not suggesting that having strong ambitions or talents rules out happiness and success, but I think we are sometimes shallow in our definitions.

Success, to me, is marrying up the things you love to do with the ability to make a living from them. What would you do, if you could do anything? Can a living be made from this? (Is the 'love of work' such a far-fetched notion?)

Who says you must accept promotions?

It's easy to feel that there must be something wrong with us for not wanting someone else's vision of success. Peer pressure combined with a shaky self-image can mean that people accept career moves and advice without even having the confidence to say 'I need to think it over!' You need to consult with your own heart and mind. Maybe this direction feels right for you. Maybe you *do* want promotion or a change in responsibility. But maybe you don't. (Maybe you'll get there and change your mind.)

This is not to say that you won't face consequences for knocking back an offer. It could be that someone feels disappointed and hesitates to consider you for future roles.

But you're certainly entitled to think things through and make your own choices.

Consider this: the end result of promotion can be a 'divorce' from the thing that you most love doing. Add to this loss the stress of being expected to perform in an entirely new role called management, often without training or development. Not everyone makes a good manager. **Management is a profession**. Not everyone is attracted to it.

'Success' can make for very unhappy people. It can result in managers hanging around their front-line staff, appearing to be interfering in details because they don't know how to say, 'Can I do this for a while? I miss it. It was something that made me happy.'

It's *very* easy to lose sight of the target. **Money is only a means to an end.** Promotion is a means to an end. It is folly to set yourself up for the idea that promotion is the only worthwhile option. There is only so much room on the corporate ladder and that same ladder is SHRINKING. Organizations are cutting layers and killing titles. It's time for a rethink, for everyone.

Every new job is a chance to start over.

It's an easy time to be writing this. Generation X and the climate of change have done a great job turning a lot of career expectations and working myths upside down.

Amongst the emerging media celebrities in Britain in the last few years have been landscape gardeners, chefs, front-line airline staff and home handymen.

I wonder if there's ever been an easier time to earn a little respect for choosing to pursue the kind of work that you love.

Every new job is a chance to start over. Any day of the year is a good enough day to grab hold of your life and plan to make some changes. It's important to plan but don't forget that it's *your* plan.

You don't have to choose a job title and stick with it for life. You're not unstable or immature because you want to change direction. To find the work that is right for you, you need a set of questions that will refine the search. You have to make the time to go through them with as much honesty and insight as you can muster. You need helpful advice from other people, but you must sift it carefully. You need to set your expectations realistically. The search won't be straightforward or without frustration. The goal posts may move a little too, as you, your circumstances and the job market will change.

You'll need patience and persistence, but don't be talked out of trying. It is never too late to try again, nor is it vain or selfish to want a working life that comes somewhere close to your aspirations.

And finally, if you stumble a bit or face some setbacks, recognize them as a part of the process.

Failure is not as frightening as regret.

Recommended reading

Behaviour/psychology

The references to the Internal and External Locus of Control originate with Julian B. Rotter, whose questions to us all were: Do we believe that our behaviour affects the outcome? Do we attribute what happens to us to factors within our control or to external factors outside of our control?

His work can be found in *Social Learning and Clinical Psychology* (Prentice Hall, 1954).

Gavin de Becker's *The Gift of Fear* (Bloomsbury, 2000) is one of the most sensible and useful books I have ever read about human behaviour, as is Steve Biddulph's *The Secret of Happy Children* (HarperCollins, 1999).

Thomas Harris's excerpt on personal change comes from the well-known *I'm OK – You're OK*, published by Galahad Books (1999). I also want to mention Dr Eric Berne and Dr Albert Ellis. Berne's work on ego states, games and transactional analysis has had such an enormous impact on my working life, as has Ellis's rational emotive therapy.

All of these writers have shared genuinely helpful insights into life and all the guff that goes with it.

Small business start-up

Small business start-ups can get advice at **www.business link. gov.uk – The No Nonsense Guide to Setting up a Business.**

Books you might find useful include:

Caspian Woods, *From Acorns…How to Build your Brilliant Business from Scratch* (Prentice Hall, 2004). A simple but smart guide to starting your own business from scratch

Steve Parks, *Start Your Business Week by Week* (Prentice Hall, 2005). A step-by-step start-up guide

Downshifting

A very useful guide to downshifting is the Dominguez and Robin guide, *Your Money or Your Life* (G. P. Putnam's Sons, 1999).

The Prudential offers a means for deciding whether you can afford to downshift at **www.pru.co.uk/home/calculator/ downshift**

You might find Carmel McConnell's *Make Money, Be Happy* (Prentice Hall, 2005) useful too.